WHAT PEOPLE ARE S.

A MYSTIC GUIDE T(
& CLEARING

A solid, well written little manual on the arcane arts of clearing
and purification. From making a wand, broom, or talisman, to
cleansing your body, aura and home, this book is presented in a
practical style that makes it easy to master. Learn about uncrossing baths, house clearing, curse breaking, and the specific
herbs and stones that will aid you in the work. Includes the care
and feeding of familiars, and spiritual relationships with
ancestors, angels, goddesses, gods and ghosts. I even identified a
new spirit animal just by reading this book!

Ellen Evert Hopman, author of *A Legacy of Druids – conversations
with Druid leaders from Britain, Canada and the USA, Past and
Present, Secret Medicines from Your Garden,* and other volumes

A Mystic Guide to Cleansing and Clearing is full of commonsense
insight and offers great techniques for ridding your life of
energies that don't serve you. I love that this book speaks to
magic users in a non tradition-specific voice, making the ideas in
this book easy to adapt to your own path. I found myself
working with some of David Salisbury's techniques before I was
even halfway through reading it. This is the kind of book that
you'll come back to again and again when the chips are down
and you need some thoughtful advice to keep the energies in
your life running smoothly.

Mickie Mueller, Illustrator, author of *Voice of the Trees* and *The
Witch's Mirror*

David Salisbury has created a helpful little book of practical
cleansing techniques, packed full of useful information. In clear,
straightforward prose he leads the reader through sensible

cleansing techniques that begin with the body and work outward to living and work spaces. He also includes an aspect that is sadly lacking in many works: how to maintain a 'spiritual hygiene' practice that will prevent future problems from arising. With no melodrama and plenty of real-life examples, Salisbury offers the reader a valuable guide to all kinds of spiritual cleansing, a resource worth returning to over and over again.

Laura Perry, author of *Ariadne's Thread: Awakening the Wonders of the Ancient Minoans in Our Modern Lives*

David Salisbury's *A Mystic Guide to Cleansing & Clearing* is a really good, down-to-earth, practical introduction to everything you need to know about cleansing your self or your working space when working with energy. Full of practical hints, recipes and tips, it is clear this is not just an ordinary how-to book – David knows his stuff from years of practical application. Accessible and very readable, I would recommend this book to anyone seeking to expand their own repertoire of cleansing rituals.

Rebecca Beattie, author of *Nature Mystics: The Literary Gateway to Modern Paganism*

David Salisbury has taken the inbuilt need we all have to clear and cleanse our inner and outer worlds, broken it down into its component parts and rebuilt it for us. In the process he has provided us with tools ranging from sprays and baths to besom brooms, soul alignment and pretty much everything in between. I found much in *A Mystic Guide to Cleansing & Clearing* that was new to me, techniques I am now impatient to try out and perhaps add to my own toolkit, for that's what is provided here, tools we can assimilate into our own practice, whatever that may be.

Yvonne Ryves, shamanic and energy healer, author of *Shaman Pathways: Web of Life*

I had the distinct honor of having David Salisbury perform a ritual cleansing on me several years ago after I felt a once-close friend had cursed me. The working left an impression that has forever followed me through my exploration in the craft. *A Mystic Guide to Cleansing & Clearing* contains the wisdom used that afternoon along with so many other treasures. A jewel for those who are looking for a direct answer in times when energy may not be at its best, this book has no problem talking about ancestral curses or entities. Salisbury is a real witch who blends the old and the new in a way that makes this work a true triumph of the modern arts.

Devin Hunter, author of *The Witch's Book of Power*

A Mystic Guide to Cleansing & Clearing

A Mystic Guide to Cleansing & Clearing

David Salisbury

Winchester, UK
Washington, USA

First published by Moon Books, 2016
Moon Books is an imprint of John Hunt Publishing Ltd., Laurel House, Station Approach,
Alresford, Hants, SO24 9JH, UK
office1@jhpbooks.net
www.johnhuntpublishing.com
www.moon-books.net

For distributor details and how to order please visit the 'Ordering' section on our website.

Text copyright: David Salisbury 2015

ISBN: 978 1 78279 623 7
Library of Congress Control Number: 2016934234

A CIP catalogue record for this book is available from the British Library.

Design: Stuart Davies

Printed and bound by CPI Group (UK) Ltd, Croydon, CR0 4YY, UK

We operate a distinctive and ethical publishing philosophy in all
areas of our business, from our global network of authors to
production and worldwide distribution.

CONTENTS

Dedication

To my grandmother Ardith, who always made sure there was a piece of candy ready to reward my cleaning work. Positive reinforcement works well when you have a sweet tooth.

Introduction

As spiritual or magical people, we often like to believe that the world is filled with light and love, ready to support our every desire. We walk through life knowing that the forces and powers around us are available to tap into and use for all our needs both large and small. I see proof of these powers every day in my life and am constantly seeking to take advantage of the many blessings that surround me each day. In many ways, the universe truly is conspiring to support us.

But sometimes the universe is not conspiring to support us. Sometimes people do terrible things to each other. Sometimes we walk through life's mud and tread it all over our brand-new white carpet. Most of us know that the crud that comes along with living is inevitable. We also have a tendency to forget that we do have a say in how we deal with the crud when it comes our way.

The options are simple: you can take charge of your life or you can be stepped on. Whether it's by people, situations, or energies, the same two choices are always presented. We may not be able to control the garbage that comes our way, but we can deal with it with wisdom and power. Making the right choices is easier said than done. Many of us have become accustomed to being stepped on in different areas in life. Many of us largely ignore it or brush it off as simply going along with the territory of living. Some of us may even think we deserve bad treatment! Maybe it's time to break the pattern.

Cleansing unhelpful energies is just as much an internal process as it is an external one. We need to look inside ourselves and uncover any patterns and complexes that might be drawing the crud our way. Only then can we wisely look around us and figure out where else it might be coming from. This book will approach both methods, giving us a holistic and balanced approach to cleansing and clearing. There are other cleansing books out there that focus on the cleansing practices of specific spiritual traditions around the globe. While I'll touch on many of those and draw inspiration from their practices, I've endeavored to create methods of cleansing that are specifically suitable to the modern-day witch and magick-worker. This means that we'll mostly stay away from cleansing methods that use tools like psalms, Christian prayer, or others from the monotheistic mindset. There is already plenty of reading material on those methods (see the appendix) and it's high time we have options aligned with Pagan thought.

This book can be used as a complete system or as a compendium of individual methods. If you're looking to incorporate the whole width of cleansing techniques into your spiritual practice, you may want to do all of the workings from start to finish. You can also simply open up a page with a spell, ritual, or other exercise that speaks to you and perform it right away. This is by no means a definitive work on the subject of cleansing and clearing, but it should arm you with the tools necessary to get started with this work and inspire you to continue it beyond this book.

Now, let's roll up our sleeves, pick up our brooms, and get to work!

Chapter 1

Cleansing Tools

My first teacher, Miss Tina, once told me: 'Tools are the icing on the cake.' I don't think she meant that they are in any way unnecessary, but that they're given to us to add richness to the deep well of power that magickal people draw from by virtue of their very nature. You can absolutely perform cleansing procedures on your own, and you should! A well-skilled mystic should be able to cleanse and clear without any tools whatsoever. After all, we never really know the types of situations we'll find ourselves in.

Tools are helpful because they speak to the subconscious in a way that raw actions usually cannot. In the psychological sense tools are symbols because they represent the ability to perform an added task that is learned through basic human evolution. When early humans learned how to use tools for building things like shelters, weapons and fires, humanity began to grow by leaps and bounds. It is for these reasons that tools have a certain power and prominence that cannot be understated. Picking up a tool for mystical purposes declares to the mind that 'something magickal is happening'. It's a trigger that is essential for propelling the mind into an alternate state of consciousness that's essential for magickal acts.

The following are descriptions of tools used for cleansing and clearing that I've come to know and love throughout my years as a mystic and witch. It is by no means exhaustive and I highly encourage you to research tools used by many spiritual traditions all over the world that you may find useful for your own personal practice.

The Broom (Besom)
In magickal practice, the word 'besom' is often used inter-

changeably with 'broom', although besom is the word used to describe any broom that is made with traditional folk methods. For our purposes here, the besom is the type of broom used by the magick-worker for sacred and mystical purposes only. In the traditional way, the handle is made from branches of hazel while the brush part is made from birch twigs bundled together. Hazel is the tree of enchantment and is widely known as being a plant favored by witches. Birch is the tree of beginnings and can be seen as a plant to bring in a fresh start to things. An alternative has the handle made of ash, which is sacred to the faery people of Celtic lore, with the brush made of willow branch ends, sacred to the Goddess and the powers of water. Some prefer a handle of oak, a tree most prized by the Druids as being the most powerful of all. Oak is also sacred to Zeus and Odin, the kings of their pantheons. The symbolism of the broom is special as the phallic shape of the handle and vulvic shape of the brush remind us of the importance of honoring the sacred power present within both sexes.

Obviously the broom has longstanding associations with witches thanks to Hollywood and modern art of American and European Halloween lore. Interestingly, the broom's connection with witchcraft extends much further than its partnership with the hook-nosed hags of the modern October celebrations. Witches have been connected with flight for hundreds of years, at least since the 16th century. Earlier stories show witches riding on common kitchen tools such as soup spoons and forks. Later images show them riding on tools like the pitchfork, and then finally the broom. The witch trials of early modern Europe claimed that witches used these tools to fly to the sabbath, the diabolical meeting grounds of the Devil who they would meet and copulate with in exchange for their infernal powers. In reality, the broom is more often used for what most think of as its intended purpose: cleaning!

Although you can obtain a traditional besom from any

number of Pagan vendors or online retailers specializing in traditional brooms, I recommend you make your own if you can. Handmade tools tend to pack a stronger punch since there's an intimacy that grows from creating something out of nothing with your bare hands. All you need to do is obtain a branch from any sacred wood as your handle. Here are some ideas:

Alder: Storms
Apple: Healing and love
Ash: Faery magick, dreams, visions
Birch: Beginnings and new homes
Blackthorn: Expels the worst curses
Cedar: Earth energy
Elm: Stability and grounding
Fir: Clarity and perspective
Hawthorn: Protection
Hazel: Lunar magick
Holly: Resurrection, resurgence, and second chances
Oak: Horned gods, success, and stability
Pine: Purification
Rowan: Protection against enchantments
Willow: Lunar magick, goddesses, and adaptability

Simply hold the branch for your staff (which should be about the length of the ground to your heart) and bind your brush material with twine, yarn, or rope. Make sure the knot is tight since you may need your besom for intense future cleansings! Bless and empower your besom with prayers and energetic workings appropriate to your personal tradition. My favorite method is to sprinkle the staff and brush of the besom with blessed salt water while under the light of a bright full moon. I may say something along the lines of:

Handle to brush and brush to ground

sweep all illness outward bound
with cunning sight and speed
this besom is blessed and so the deed.

It is often recommended that the besom is swept with a west to east motion, following the course of the setting sun. Although when you're using it on a house with many rooms and floors, that can get a little confusing. I think it's fine to sweep any way that seems sensible for the room. I do, however, urge you to sweep in the direction of the doorway to the room that you are in. Instead of simply stirring up and disrupting negative energies, you want them to actually vacate the room and your home, so this is important.

Your besom's brush bristles don't actually need to touch the physical floor to sweep out energy. I like to imagine sparks of blue flame shooting from the tips of the brush blades as I sweep about 3-6 inches above the surface of the floor. As I do this, I imagine the pockets of negative energy being forcibly bound up and brushed aside with every sweeping motion.

Knowing the basics of besom cleansing, get creative with how you do your sweeping. Try a regular routine of besom cleansing where you 'sweep out' unhelpful energies right after you finish the chore of actually sweeping up dirt. If you have hardwood floors, try laying down a cleansing powder and sweeping that up along with the dirt before you begin your besom cleansing. This is a fun cleansing method for families since kids are given permission to make a mess, and then tasked with mindfully cleaning it up right after. You could even make a game out of it!

The Wand

The history of the wand in magick is even more widespread than the besom. Everyone from the priests of ancient Egypt to the ceremonial magicians of the Renaissance used magickal wands in one form or another. The wand is a symbol of sovereignty and represents the holder's authority over the self and their environment. It is a representation of the will and an energetic extension of the arm, showing the magick-worker's 'reach' into the otherworld. This sentiment is still seen in the rods and scepters carried by certain members of royalty in kingdoms throughout the world. And although those rods are more symbolic than anything, it shows how the power of the wand has survived in its prominence. We can think of it like the trunk of a tree or the stem of a plant, as a conduit connecting different types of energy and acting as a channel for them.

To craft your own wand, all you need to do is find a small fallen branch of the wood you like and cut it so it's the length of your elbow to the tip of your middle finger. It can really be any size you desire, but this is the standard length in many traditions and tends to feel the most comfortable for most people. Next, you'll want to perform any physical changes to it you want like shaving off parts of the bark, sanding it down, and even finishing it with a paint or enamel if you like. Most of these changes will be cosmetic, but I do think there is a certain power in personalizing the wand to make it your own. After that, bless the wand by whispering your intentions into it and making an offering to the tree spirit you took it from. A cup of blessed water is fine. A wand used specifically for clearing, banishing, and even cursing is called a 'blasting rod'. You may find it useful to have a wand that acts solely as your blasting rod and using it only for that purpose.

The power of the wand as a show of sovereignty and authority is what we're concerned with when we talk about cleansing work. This is especially so in the case of entity moving and removal. There are all kinds of interesting stories about magicians pointing a wand at a spirit or demon as it flees away in submission. Though I hope you'll never have to use a wand for such a thing, it's certainly handy to have it around in any case. I've found that pockets of negative energy in general will also have the same reaction, although you should put your own effort and energy into it as well, rather than just relying on the wand itself.

To use a wand in cleansing, first point it at the area. For a room cleansing, I will stand in the doorway of the room and point it towards the middle of the room in the center of the floor. Feel the power build up inside you in the form of glistening blue fire. Allow the fire to flow out through your arm and into the wand. Feel the flame becoming concentrated until at last it blasts out to the center of the room. The fire swirls about and disintegrates any and all negative energies in its path. You should use a little caution with this method when practicing it on a person, as the blast of blue fire can be a little harsh to experience. For a personal cleansing, I like to slowly wave it all around the person, like a metal detector wand, feeling any unhelpful energies flying off the person as the wand makes its way around the subject's energy bodies.

You can also use a wand to 'carry' energies to a better place for the purpose of transmuting them into something helpful. For example, let's say you just had an argument with a family member or roommate. You feel that the argument let a lot of things off both your chests and will ultimately lead to healing, but you don't really want the heavy and intense post-argument feeling to stay lingering in the air. Take your wand to the room(s) where the argument was held and slowly wave it counter-clockwise in the air. As you do this, imagine that the words of the argument are swirling around the room like a dirty tornado. As the words gather together, see them being drawn towards the tip of the wand as if it were the point of a powerful magnet attracting metal flecks. Once you feel the memory of the argument attached to the wand, drag it outdoors. You may like to drag it completely off the bounds of your property, although I don't think that's really necessary. Point the wand to the ground and begin tapping the soil with the wand, seeing the words of the argument pour into the earth. Next, you can draw up power from the earth in the same way you drew up the memory of the argument. Carry this energy back into your home and into the room(s). Wave the wand around the room clockwise and feel the calming earth energies disperse into the environment around you. Clearing methods like this allow you to take control of a bad situation and turn it into an opportunity for empowerment and healing.

Be sure to get creative with not only the making of your wand, but in the use of it too. Anything that requires a strong will will be well aided by the use of a wand.

Musical Instruments

Bells, gongs, chimes, drums, and singing bowls all have a rich history in traditions of spiritual cleansing. Sound in general is another powerful method of triggering a shift in consciousness in our minds. Ringing a bell before a ritual act is like pushing a 'reset' button in my mind. It's an invitation to bring an end to whatever I was doing before I begin whatever sacred act I'm about to engage in. This is why so many spiritual traditions feature the ringing of bells and the striking of gongs before and after a ceremony. Catholics who come to Wicca later in life will often talk about feeling soothed by the memory of bells, since that practice exists in both faiths. Traditional magick-workers such as witches will ring a bell at the beginning and end of a spell to open the way for power to flow correctly from the start to the finish.

Bells are an easy way to begin incorporating sound into your cleansing practice. There are so many different kinds of hand-held bells so you'll need to pick one that has a pitch that matches the type of energy you want to attract and/or drive away. Bigger bells with a lower pitch are good for general cleansing and 'neutralizing' the atmosphere. This is the type of bell you might use to signal the beginning of other types of cleansing or any other ceremonial work. They might remind you of the old church bells in your town that ring at specific intervals to signal the change in time throughout the day. Smaller bells with a higher pitch will raise the vibration of a room, making it difficult for negative energies that operate on a lower frequency to exist. As the Hermetic law of vibration states, the overpowering presence of something with a high vibration will always cancel out something with a lower vibration.

An easy method of cleansing with bells is to take one to each corner of a room and give it an enthusiastic ring three times. Do this in every corner of every room in your home. If you're in a hurry and need to cleanse quickly, you can just give it a ring in the center of each room instead. You can also pair each ringing with some kind of spoken declaration like: 'Toll of the bell signals my spell that all evil shall quell!' Another easy way to use bells is to put them in areas of the home where they'll ring on their own. Attach a bell to your front door so it rings every time it's opened and closed, like the bells of a small storefront. You can also attach one to your cat's collar so every movement of your feline companion is accompanied with a gentle jingle.

Tuning forks take the idea of a bell's vibration a step further. They're very common among the new age and alternative healing communities and you can find elaborate themed sets of them online and in many metaphysical stores. The idea of the forks are the same as the bell, but the forks will have single, long frequencies when struck. The long resounding tone allows a long wave of vibration to be sent through the air to affect more places than many of the bell methods. Different types of tuning forks are associated with different systems including body parts, parts of the soul, emotions, states of consciousness, states of evolution, and chakras. In the chakra system, forks with lower tunes belong to the root chakra. The higher the pitch of a fork, the higher up the chakra, until you get to the highest pitch tone at the crown chakra. Although I don't own a set of tuning forks myself, I have received a chakra cleansing by tuning forks and I could strongly feel the vibration of the tones purifying and recharging the chakras from bottom to top. Complete sets of the forks can be pricey, but if you have a strong interest in chakra balancing and aura cleansing through sound, it's probably worth the investment.

To use tuning forks for clearing space, try accompanying the pitch of the fork to an intention that you vocally intone. Match the pitch of your singing voice to the pitch of the fork. Strike the fork and intone loudly: 'I clear this space by the highest vibrations of the universe!' To cleanse a space with lower, soothing frequencies, strike a low-pitch fork and intone loudly: 'I clear this space by the deep vibrations of the earth!' For clearing unhelpful energies from the body, strike the fork as close to the skin as you can and imagine waves of vibrational energy rumbling through the entire physical body and out through the other end. Some people even believe that certain pitches of tuning forks can actually heal DNA in the body, restoring it to the most perfect state of health possible.

Wind chimes offer a great way to combine all types of pitches of sound. My only suggestion with hanging chimes is that you should use chimes that are at a similar level of pitch. Either have all high-pitch sets of wind chimes or all low-pitch sets. Listening to a mixture of high and low tones all the time all at once can make the energy of a space feel cluttered and chaotic. I don't think the combination generates harmful vibrations, but I tend to stay away from things that feel annoying and distortive. That said, if you have a genuine love of hearing the clamoring sounds of different pitches all at once, then by all means ignore that advice. Cleansing, as with most forms of energy manipulation, is a deeply personal experience.

Finally, you may wish to experiment with drums, rattles, and other types of percussion instruments. The theory behind cleansing drum beats is the same as the bells and chimes. Specifically, there is something deeply soothing about hearing a deep drum beat that follows the rate of a human heartbeat. This is the sound we heard in our mother's womb before we were even born so hearing this frequency inspires a shift in consciousness back to one of pure awe and love. Bang out a drum beat to match the rhythm of a slow heartbeat to instill your environment with the powers of goddess energy and the renewing energies of gestation and birth. This is a great cleansing method for springtime when the new shoots of plants are just starting to push up through the ground in your area.

Feathers, Bones, and Animal Curios

The discarded remnants of animals resonate with the natural powers of that animal's totem. I say 'discarded' because we should always look for animal tools that were given freely through shedding, or the natural death process. An animal should never be killed with the intention of using his or her body as a tool because that tool will then be desecrated with the memory of a needless killing at human hands. Feathers can be found quite easily, along with bones from animals who have naturally died and decomposed in woods and fields. Observe strict caution when harvesting animal parts because you may be exposing yourself to bacteria harmful to human health. I advise you to wear protective gloves and then sterilize the parts with bleach and hot soapy water as soon as possible. Keep in mind that it is illegal in certain countries or states to possess the feathers of endangered birds, regardless of how you came across them.

You may already be familiar with feathers as a way of spreading the smoke of incense or a smudge stick for cleansing. You can also use feathers on their own, without any other material. As you walk through the space or around the person you are clearing, hold the feather with your projective hand and sense the spirit of the bird it belonged to. What does that bird look like when he or she is in the heights of flight? What is the sound of his or her call? What energies does the bird possess? Here's a brief list of common properties and powers associated with birds:

Blackbird: Determination and tenacity
Bluebird: Happiness, contentment, inner peace
Cardinal: Vitality, brilliance, health
Chicken: Fertility, promises, kindness
Crow: Wisdom, witchcraft, cunning, death, spirits
Dove: Peace, prophecy, instinct
Duck: Emotional balance and discernment
Eagle: Insight, travel, leadership
Falcon: Agility and timeliness
Goose: Imagination and cooperation
Hawk: Communication and observation
Magpie: Omens and prophecy
Owl: Understanding, moon magick, strategy
Peacock: Watchfulness, sovereignty, spiritual integration
Pheasant: Family
Rooster: Protection
Raven: Battle, the otherworld, psychic power
Sparrow: Dignity and self-worth
Swan: Transition and spiritual evolution
Vulture: Transmutation and creating a good thing out of a bad thing

If you can't obtain the type of feather you like, whether out of legal constraints or practical ones, simply call upon the spirit of the bird to come to your aid during your cleansing work. You can even hold a feather of some other kind and ask the bird you need to infuse the feather with its own essence.

Bones are the gemstones of our ancestors, both animal and human alike. The idea behind using bones is similar to using feathers, although you are specifically tapping into the death current of the animal or person. I include humans in this category because it is possible to purchase human bones from online storefronts or specialty curio shops. Again, the laws vary in the type of bones you're allowed to have depending on your country.

Since bones resonate with the power of death and the memory of our ancestors, we can use bones for cleansing work that requires the backup of our spirit allies. This is what I call 'big guns' work and is something I'll do when I need to clear out a powerful and stubborn force. Exorcisms could be greatly aided by a bone, along with the removal of a mischievous discarnate spirit on your property. Some people believe that it is enough to just wave a bone at a spirit to send it away. Others may carve it into a knife or wand to use as a consistent ritual tool, which can be marked up and adorned like other 'standard' ritual tools.

Censer

The censer is the container you will use to burn cleansing agents such as herbs, resins, papers, powders, and oils. The use of the censer extends back into the far mists of time, in the temples of old around the world. If you've ever been to a classic Catholic mass, you'll be familiar with the swinging of the incense censer during the recitations of prayers. Censers come in all shapes and sizes for all types of use. The abalone shell is a common choice for smudge sticks. The classic stick incense burner is the most commonly available, although any heat-proof container will work. For anything other than stick incense (where the heat source doesn't really come into contact with the container much), you need a thick container to prevent heat transfer. I like to use a sturdy porcelain and stone bowl that I'll also fill up with sand or salt. Bases like this will absorb the heat and prevent unfortunate accidents like the scorching of countertops and floors.

My preferred type of censer is a cauldron. Although I also use cauldrons to hold liquids for mixing fluids, my cauldron is an excellent container for things that need burning. Since they're usually made of cast iron, they hold heat well and you don't have to worry about fires and coals scorching them beyond repair. I also like cauldrons because they have a spiritual resonance that I will also call upon during my work. Cauldrons are an old tool of transformation and empowerment in several cultures (the Celtic peoples in particular) and their mythos provides us with a great way to access potent powers for our cleansing work. The famous cauldron of Cerridwen from Wales is probably the best known example of the cauldron of transformation. In the story, the witch-goddess Cerridwen hired an assistant to stir her potion of inspiration every day. When three drops splashed out of the cauldron, turning its potion to poison, Cerridwen became enraged and chased her assistant around the world in various forms. At last the assistant transformed into a piece of grain and was gobbled up by the angry goddess, who had transformed herself into a hen. He was then reborn through her, giving us an inspiring tale of risk and transformation.

Cleansing objects is an example of something to use a censer for. In your censer, burn your cleansing herbs appropriate to what you're doing and wave the object over it. If there's room in the censer and you're not worried about getting the object ashy and inflamed, you can leave it in there and close the lid over it. Wait a moment and then open the lid to release a big puff of the cleansing smoke into the air. Don't you just love it when spiritual work is theatrical?

Aspergillum

Asperging is the ritual act of cleansing and blessing something with water. Again we can use the example of the Catholic Church, which uses the aspergillum (in its case it typically looks like a rod with a metallic ball at the end) to throw holy water on an area or person. Some of these tools have a sponge inside them so that the holy water is self-contained. Others have to be dipped into a container holding the water called an aspersorium. These funny words have a direct and simple meaning: from the Latin word 'aspergere', which means 'to sprinkle'. I suppose you could also just call it a 'sacred sprinkler', but we mystics do love our fancy Latin names. The Bible discusses an aspergillum made from cedar wood and hyssop, which is interesting since these two plants have a long history of cleansing and clearing in other spiritual practices as well.

The aspergillum is a common tool on the altar in many different Wiccan traditions and is typically placed near the chalice and bowl of salt. They can really be made out of anything, although many Pagans prefer a natural material like a loosely bound bundle of twigs or leaves. My favorite type of aspergillum is fresh, leafy rosemary stems that are bound together at one end. The many different little leaves enable the bundle to hold water well and rosemary is a powerful and ancient herb for purification on its own. For a powerful cleansing rite, you could asperge an area with the rosemary bundle and let the rosemary dry, then burn that later in the censer. A bundle of rue tied together at one end would also make an excellent aspergillum, especially for the removal of hexes and curses.

Exercise: Making Holy Water

Now that you know how to use the aspergillum, you need some holy water to go with it. Making holy water is one of my most favorite things to teach people how to do. There's an assumption that only members of the clergy (in any faith) can make it. Wrong! It is your divine right as a human being to cleanse what needs to be cleansed and to bless what needs to be blessed.

Holy water will be one of your core methods of clearing away energies and blessing space, objects, and yourself. Its simple ingredients and method of creation mean that you can make it just about anywhere, from your own kitchen to a hotel room to a restaurant dinner table.

Materials:
Water
Salt

Put some clean water (distilled or spring water is best, but any clean water will do) into a bowl and make sure you have the salt close by. Set the bowl of water before you and begin to enter a meditative state by breathing slowly and deeply, focusing on releasing any tension in the body with the breath. In your mind's eye, imagine that a brilliant white light is beginning to stir from inside your body. Using your imagination, feel that light growing rapidly upon every breath until it spreads throughout your full body, concentrating most brilliantly into your arms and hands.

Slide your hands back and forth rapidly, feeling the heat from the friction between them. As you do, the light from your body flows quickly into the space between your hands until there is a magnificent shining sphere of energy before you. Once you feel like you can raise no more energy this way, place your hands palms down over the bowl of water and imagine all of the light flowing into it. As the light penetrates the surface of the water, it takes on its own hue of shining white and electric blue. Leave your hands over the water until you feel that all of the light has flowed into the water.

Take seven pinches of salt and sprinkle them into the water, stirring the mixture up with your index finger.

With your finger still dipped into the water, begin to trace spirals into the water, moving clockwise. The clockwise spiral pulls in energy and symbolizes the mysteries of rebirth, which represent some of the most powerful and sacred forces known to humanity. Invoking the spiral here awakens the inner power of the salt and calls forth its ability to cleanse and purify all that it touched. Combined with the charged up water, it triggers a catalyst for the dual forces of creation and destruction, birth and death, time and eternity, and darkness and light.

After tracing the sacred spirals for a couple of minutes, pick up the bowl and bring it close to your face and whisper a blessing into it. The act of whispering a blessing is how I was trained to make holy water, although this part varies wildly. I find it best to make up your own words that describe your intention for the water. If you'd like to use some words of mine, try this:

I consecrate thee, oh creature of water
that you may purify and bless all that you touch.
May the primordial forces of the universe awaken for my blessing
and flow into this vessel.
Blessed be!

Your brand new holy water is now ready to go! Use this to asperge your space, anoint your body, rub on your tools, or really anything else you can think of.

Scourge

Scourging, or ritual whipping, is a practice in British Traditional Wicca including the Gardnerian and Alexandrian traditions. The purpose of the scourge is not to cause physical harm, but to bring the blood gently to the surface of the skin, causing a slight shift in consciousness and the raising of power. In the *Book of Shadows*, Gardner states:

Ask the Goddess to help you to obtain your desires, then Scourge
again to bind the spell. This be powerful in ill luck and for sickness.
It must be said in a Circle, and you must be properly prepared and
well purified, both before and after saying, to bind the spell. Before
starting you must make a very clear picture in your mind of what
you wish. Make yourself see the wish obtained. Be sure in your own
mind exactly what it is and how it is to be fulfilled.

The scourge is not only used to manifest the desires of the magick-worker, but also to purify the body. To practice ritual scourging yourself, try bundling together nylon cord or rope into nine concentric loops that are wrapped together to form a sort of homemade cat-of-nine-tails. State your intentions to the powers that be, that you wish to be purified of all that binds you from your full potential. The Gardnerian *Book of Shadows* suggests a light whipping of your back around 40 times to 'make the skin tingle.' It's the altered state of consciousness that triggers the mind into a 'cleansing state' where lower vibrations of thought patterns cannot exist.

Plants

Plants have their own dedicated section later in this book. Plants can be used for all types of cleansing work such as burning, asperging, blasting, knocking, and more. The power of plants and trees has always been known in the ancient world in the cleansing arena. Most of us are familiar with Moses' staff, which was used to banish the serpents of the Egyptian priests who challenged him. This rod, made of wood, later became Aaron's rod, which is probably one of the best known pieces of magickal woods used for cleansing and banishment in the world. On an entirely different note, we can also think of the apple that was given to Eve by the serpent as a type of cleansing plant. Instead of being bound to the illusion of perfection, Eve ate the apple and claimed the power of lust and love, driving away the false facade of her surrounding and driving the world into a state of advancement. Biblical scholars would consider that version of the story a stretch, but as a Pagan, my position on this 'fall' is clear.

A good mystic with a cleansing practice should consider keeping a stock of basic herbs to assist in this work. We've already talked about the use of herbs burned in censers and sprinkled as an aspergent. If it's not already obvious, I'm a huge fan of using herbs for the work of cleansing. Throughout this book you'll see many recipes for potions, brews, bath mixes, incense, and floor washes that use a wide variety of herbs. The herbs known for cleansing have largely ancient back stories, with many newcomers in the world of cleansing. It can be hard to decide which are the right ones to choose for your work. I tend to go with whatever I have on hand, sometimes experimenting with different herbs that are harder to find when I can.

Developing a relationship with the spirits of the plants you're working with is the best way to gain their considerable power for your work. Many of us are familiar with the concept of animal spirits, but we often ignore the importance of working with the spirits of plants. I find that plant spirits actually tend to be easier to work with than animal spirits. Plants are mostly stationary, except when their seeds are being carried away by weather and animals. Their subtle changes make it easier to approach them and ask for guidance.

The best way to form relationships with plant spirits is to grow them yourself if you can. Rosemary is one of the easiest plants to grow and will usually thrive even when kept indoors on a sunny window ledge. All of the mints are even easier to grow and are wonderful for clearing away feelings of poverty and despair. When planting your herbs, simply enter a meditative state and feel your mind 'entering' the seed, stem, or root of the plant. Ask its permission to meld its energy with yours. Give the plant some of your energy while informing it that you intend to begin a working relationship that will hopefully be mutually beneficial for the both of you. Once the plant is in the ground, make sure to speak with it frequently and give little bits of your energy here and there.

In cleansing and clearing, you'll be working both with fresh and dried plants. That's why it's helpful to have live, growing plants on hand as well as jars and bags of herbs that you purchase dry or dry yourself. While the medicinal properties of plants tend to expire after a year, I believe that their mystical properties exist forever. Their powers are embedded into the DNA of the plant.

Divination Tools

Divination is the art of using tools to see into the beyond, whether it is past, present, or future. While you may think of tools like tarot cards and pendulums as useful only for fortune telling, they can tell you a lot about the condition of a person or place before you begin a cleansing working.

Most people are familiar with pendulums and their ability to easily answer 'yes' and 'no' types of questions. My favorite use is detecting subtle shifts of energy around the home or within a person. Pendulums are great tools to start out with because they can pick up on things happening in very specific areas that would go largely unnoticed by tarot or the runes. Before clearing a house, simply walk through every room and look for changes in a pendulum's speed and direction. You'll probably find pockets of places that make the pendulum either act erratically or completely stop. A wildly spinning pendulum usually means there's a buildup of chaotic energy that needs to be broken up. A stale pendulum can indicate an area that has stagnant energy that needs to move around. Figuring out areas like this ahead of time can save you a lot of time and help you avoid having to immediately redo a working.

Tarot cards are excellent for looking at the specific details of a person and their life. I like to use tarot when I'm uncrossing someone because it can tell me about a variety of factors that help me make the most of my work. Is this person's condition mostly psychological? Is there something going on in their subconscious mind that's manifesting greater pockets of negative energy than what is typical for them? Look for swords cards that indicate power and aggression, which can show if there is a need for a stronger type of working. Sometimes a condition will have such a weak hold that a blast of fresh energy onto the person's energy bodies is all that's needed to solve the problem. Cups cards can show if the condition is better worked within the realm of dreams and psychic discovery. They may also show if there's an emotional root to the problem. Pentacles cards can show how long the situation has been in place and how deeply rooted the negative vibrations are in the person's energy bodies. Wands can indicate if there are multiple sources and causes for a crossed condition.

My favorite divination method, which works a little like the tarot, is the runes. The runes are an ancient Norse script that was used for everything from writing and signage to spellcasting and divination. The runes are great for looking into the specifics of any situation and the circumstances that surround it. It is said that power of the runes is limited only by human imagination, which is another reason why they're a great tool to use for uncovering and cleansing stubborn situations.

Scrying is the art of looking into a reflective or translucent surface, such as a black mirror, bowl of water, or crystal ball, to see into the past, present or future. Most people say that this is the hardest divination method to learn. But once you practice and begin to get the hang of it, scrying can be an enormous help. I like to scry when I'm working on clearing entities out of a space. I will usually gaze into my black mirror and ask that the image of the entity appear before me. If the type of entity is unknown, sometimes scrying for it will help me figure it out.

Journal

Last but not least we have the journal. Like all mystical endeavors, it's worthwhile to track your progress so you can identify the most effective practices for your work. If you have a journal you keep solely for your spiritual work like a mirror book or a book of shadows, you can use that. You could also keep a journal specifically for cleansing and clearing.

I keep all sorts of things in my cleansing journal and it's really helped my terrible memory to recall what I've done and what works for me. Whenever I go into a home for a clearing, I record any issues or activity as reported by the residents. Then I chart my plan of action, what I actually did, and the results. If you want to break it down into a format that shows all the specifics, try using this outline:

Cleansing Case Study Before Working
Date, time, moon phase:
Issue of concern:
Results of divination:
Planned actions:

After Working
Actions used:
Areas of the home/body/object covered:
Feelings and insights during the working:
Feelings and insights immediately after the working:
Feelings and insights one week after the working:

If you're performing a working for someone else, it will be important to get their take on any feelings and insights before and after the working. For a house clearing, I try to involve the clients in some way so they can feel like they own the energy of their own home. When I do that, I'll also ask them how they felt during the working. If it needs to be performed again at any point in the future, I can use my journal to look back and see what worked, what didn't, and make a plan for what I might want to do differently.

Odds, Ends, and More!
Now that you have an idea of a stock of cleansing tools, feel free to get creative! I often find little things here and there that I may want to incorporate into my workings like string, fabric,

costumes, masks, whacky instruments, and even food. Since cleansing is all about moving energy by using your own, incorporating as many different ideas as possible will be most helpful. The mystic arts are as much an art as they are a science. Through trial and error, you'll figure out which tools to keep in your cleansing arsenal, and which to ditch.

Chapter 2

Clean Body, Clean Soul

The human energy body is like a sponge. It tends to absorb the influences of everything around it. That's why it's so important to 'keep yourself clean,' as grandma might say. We all have days when we get home from work and, for one reason or another, just feel downright grimy and in need of a shower. Sure you had a great day. Sure you did your spiritual work that morning. But that's not always enough.

Our bodies are designed to be receptive. That's why we have the powers of compassion, empathy, and relation to one another. It's natural for humans to take in the energies of the environments around us. Our environment informs us and helps us make decisions about where we should go next. There's a reason why the old axiom of 'trust your intuition' is as popular as it is. A well-informed spiritual body can lead to a life of mindfulness and intention.

Unfortunately, the body can't always tell the difference between energy signatures that inform us and energies that are a threat to our own bodies. That's why it's important to have a regular practice of spiritual cleansing that includes the physical, mental, and spiritual bodies. Think of it like that saucepan you cook in all the time for dinner. When you keep it clean regularly, it's a whole lot easier to take care of. But, if you let it sit on the stove and allow the dirt and grime to build up, it's much harder to scrape the scum off the surface.

The body is a complicated landscape with many things to consider. Our thoughts, experiences, and emotions are just a few of the many conditions that the body's makeup consists of. One of the big pitfalls in personal cleansing is the issue of ignoring certain parts of the self while focusing too much on another part.

Sometimes what you think is a big emotional attachment is actually just some extra debris that a colleague may have pushed on you. Other times, there may be factors that you won't even become aware of until the energy drain is doing its work.

In her 1930 book *Psychic Self-Defense*, the great occultist Dion Fortune describes what can happen to the energy body when there's a negative energy attachment:

> My body was like an electric battery that has been completely discharged. It took a long time to charge up again, and every time it was used before the charging was completed, it ran down again rapidly. For a long time I had no reserves of energy, and after the least exertion would fall into a dead sleep at any hour of the day. In the language of occultism, the etheric double had been damaged, and leaked prana. It did not become normal until I took initiation into the occult order in which I subsequently trained. Within an hour of the ceremony I felt a change, and it is only upon the rarest occasions since then, after some psychic injury, that I have had a temporary return of those depleting attacks of exhaustion.

The first step in maintaining healthy energy bodies is to learn about what makes them tick. Let's look at some of the systems that make up the energy patterns in the body and how we can work with them for optimal psychic health.

The Three Parts of the Self

Many mystic traditions from all over the world have a multi-layered view of the soul. There are different layers and aspects of our brains, skin, and internal organs. Why shouldn't the soul be the same? In a many-soul model, the part of the self or parts of the soul work together to process different types of energies and experiences.

Soul alignment comes to us primarily by way of the Anderson Feri tradition of witchcraft. Like Feri, Firefly follows a three-soul cosmology. Meaning, we are made up of various soul parts that serve various roles in our existence. Each soul is equally valuable and the goal of soul alignment is to bring all three souls into conversation with each other. Think of it like a computer switchboard, where all portions of the program must be connected for optimal success. When our souls are aligned, we have greater access to our power, our divine nature, our base instincts, and our deep mind.

Fetch: Located around the sex regions of the body and also thought to cover the body in a thin layer right on top of the skin. Also called the Lower Self, fetch is responsible for instinct, survival, desire, hunger, ego, vitality, and all things related to the body and one's 'gut instinct'.

Talker: Located around the torso and thought to circulate the body as a sphere (the aura). Talker is our outward conscious body responsible for processing our thoughts and communicating them to the outside world. Talker tries to make sense of things, whether helpful or not. Talker is all about the personality and thrives when individuality and personal ideas are expressed.

Godsoul: Located about 6 inches above the head, or around the head as a halo or sphere. Also called the Holy Dove or Higher Self. Godsoul is our pure, perfect nature. It is everything about us that stretches towards divinity and holiness. Godsoul is responsible for our eternal connection to infinity and all contained within it. Godsoul can sometimes overburden talker and fetch, as seen in people who are too flighty or air-headed (think about the flakey hippies of SNL sketches who can't do anything in the physical world).

Soul alignment should ideally be performed on a regular basis.

You can even perform it multiple times a day if you remember to! There are many variations of the soul alignment exercise and some are lengthier than others. The shortest forms can be practiced in just a moment. Longer versions can take 10 minutes or longer. Our version is a medium length and will get faster the more you practice it.

Exercise: Soul Alignment

Begin by breathing slowly, allowing yourself to relax, muscle by muscle. As you get comfortable with the exercise, you may wish to dim the lights or even play some relaxing music. The breath is the most important thing here. You should patiently allow the breath to take you down into a relaxed and centered state.

Focus your attention on fetch. Continuing breathing, allow feelings of survival, instinct, and desire to well up within you. What is fetch telling you? What does it need? What does it have to offer? On your exhale, feel the energy of fetch expanding within and around you.

Raise your attention up to talker. Continuing to breathe, allow feelings of personal expression, worldly success (and failure), and your current place in the world to well up within you. What is talker telling you? What does it need? What does it have to offer? On your exhale, feel the energy of talker expanding within and around you.

Allow your attention rise high up into Godsoul. Continuing to breathe, allow the knowledge of your divine perfection to well up within you. You are a strong, whole, and eternal being. Know this and own it. What is Godsoul telling you? What does it need? What does it have to offer? On your exhale, feel the energy of Godsoul expanding within and around you.

Rapidly return your attention to fetch and with a sharp inhale, pull in energy to fetch and store it there. With another sharp inhale, shoot it up to talker and let it rest there. With another sharp inhale, push that energy back down to fetch.

Now, in your biggest inhale, pull in all your power to fetch. On your next exhale, tilt your head upwards and sharply exhale the breath as you vocalize (preferably shout) the sound 'HA!'

You feel the energy and breath rush up from fetch and hit Godsoul like a firework. It explodes into an ecstatic merger of power and umbrellas like a fountain above your head.

The energy then cascades down around you, like a shining waterfall of power, blessing the other souls in its descent, until it rests at last with fetch.

Repeat aloud, even if in a whisper:

Parts of self aligned as one
By rising moon and setting sun
Above, below, and middle three
Join within their unity

Breathe comfortably as you feel your souls aligned as one. If you received any insights or sensations from any of your souls, now would be a great time to record them.

Chakras

Chakra means 'wheel of light' in Sanskrit and that accurately describes what they look like. Most people have some idea of what chakras are – the points of energy in a person's body. To the mystic, they're so much more. Chakras are like the internal organs of the energy body, helping to translate the energy we encounter and generate more of it. Think of them like the microprocessors of the body's biological computer system.

Although the body actually has hundreds of chakras of varying sizes, the ones we're usually concerned with are seven major chakras that are lined up (roughly) through the center of the body. Each of these chakras performs a specific task. Being in touch with the status of each one can help us to remove any blocks or attachments that might hinder the healthy flow of energy. Here's a quick rundown of the main seven, with their nicknames and original Sanskrit names:

Crown (Sahasrara): Located a few inches above the head and surrounding the head itself. The crown chakra might also be thought of as the Godsoul in the three-soul model we just discussed. It's the most pure, perfect, and holy part of you. When the crown chakra is working well, we are transmitting divine energy and are able to send and receive information easily from spirit. When the crown is blocked or misaligned, we can feel detached from the divine powers. People with blocked crown chakras report feeling disconnected from their life's purpose and generally unable to find inspiration.

Third Eye (Anja): Located on the forehead, the third eye is the center of your psychic senses and controls the flow of dreams and mental clarity. When the third eye is in good working condition, we have the ability to see clearly in the otherworld and beyond the initial layers of conditions presented to us. When the third eye is blocked or misaligned, people will report feeling forgetful, sleepy, or in a state of general fogginess.

Throat (Visuddha): The throat chakra is the center of self-expression and creativity. Think of this chakra as the gateway between your personality and the way you express it to other people. A healthy throat chakra allows you to speak your mind to others as well as making sure you're staying true to yourself. A blocked or misaligned throat chakra can make you feel like you're not being heard by others. Others experience a sense of self-deprivation and not being able to get comfortable with their own ideas.

Heart (Anahata): The heart chakra is about everything that you think it might be about. It's your center of love, compassion, and emotion. Its traditional color is green, which reminds us that the heart is like a garden. It must be constantly tended with care and given the nutrients and exercise it needs to thrive. A blocked or misaligned heart chakra can make you feel unloved and also prevent you from loving others. It can restrict your ability to feel empathy with others, which further complicates relationships with others, whether it's with a friend, a lover, or a family member.

Solar Plexus (Manipura): I like to think of the solar plexus chakra as the power generator for all the other chakras. The other chakras rely on the solar plexus to pull the energy needed to run its entire system. A healthy solar plexus chakra makes you feel filled with vitality and joy. A blocked or misaligned solar plexus can leave you feeling weak and lethargic. Some people even report getting sick more often, as the solar plexus chakra is thought to control the immune system.

Sacral (Svadisthana): The sacral chakra is all about trust and the ability to be resilient when the energy bodies are tested. If you're one of those people who is easily able to 'bounce back' from a tough situation, you probably have a healthy sacral chakra. When this chakra is blocked or misaligned, it's harder to get out of depression states and general grief. It can also cause you to be more fearful and less willing to take risks.

Root (Muladhara): The root chakra (also called the base) is where our sense of survival is stored. If all the other chakras were suffering, the root chakra would kick in to make sure you're doing the bare minimum to stay alive. A healthy root chakra results in courage, willpower, and a general fiery outlook on life. A blocked or misaligned root chakra can make you feel cowardly or in a constant state of panic. The root chakra can sometimes be too active, causing a sense of unnecessary urgency. People who struggle with hoarding often have an overactive root chakra that needs to be calmed and balanced with the others. Its location is generally considered to be at or below the genitals.

Common Problems with Chakras

Just like the physical parts of our bodies, there are many ways that a chakra can become unhealthy. And just as it's important to know what issue is affecting a part of the physical body, it's equally important to know about issues that affect the energy bodies. This can get confusing since some psychic healers and energy workers will use the term 'blocked chakra' as a catch-all explanation for a chakra that just doesn't feel right. Many systems of clearing and healing will work out most surface issues with the chakras, but to have a deeply effective course of treatment, it's best to accurately identify what's actually going on. Here are some of the key issues that unhealthy chakras have:

Unbalanced

This is a general issue that I encounter most often when working with a client for a healing. With all of the daily stresses we encounter today, it can be very easy for a chakra to become unbalanced. Chakras become unbalanced when one or more chakras have a lesser flow of energy or other chakras have too high a flow. Often it can be a mixture of these two conditions, which throws the whole system out of whack. If a chakra is depleted of energy, the other chakras often make up for the loss by over producing more energy. For example, if the root chakra is feeling depleted, then the crown chakra might overcompensate for the loss by producing extreme feelings of needing to escape completely into the mystical world. A drained throat chakra might result in the solar plexus chakra producing tons of bombastic energy that results in feeling easily agitated and distressed.

The practice of balancing the chakras is fairly simple and can be performed on yourself or others with minimal effort most times.

Begin by scanning the body for the problem areas. I like to do this by slowly moving my hand up and down my body, a few inches above the skin. Do you notice any areas that are particularly hot or cold? Maybe some areas have a strong buzzing sensation, or lack of any sensation? This is where using your intuition and best judgment is important. Just allow the body to speak to you in its own language and sense what it's trying to say.

If you come across a chakra that seems to have too much energy or is inflamed in some way, start there. Using the energy of your hand, 'pull' the excess energy of it out and into the other parts of the body. This is where being resourceful comes in. If there are chakra areas that have a lack of energy, you can move that energy there. If one chakra is hyperactive and there are no chakras lacking, then wave the hand up and down the body, distributing the excess energy evenly throughout.

If the problem is lack of energy from the chakra and not enough excess energy to fill the gap, you can pull energy in from other sources. There are so many ways to do this. If you're a practitioner of Reiki, then that will be easy enough for you. If you're not a practitioner of an energy system like Reiki, you can draw on energy from the environment around you. During the day, you can raise your hand towards the sun and call down raw, golden energy into the chakra. If at night, figure out where the moon is and do the same with lunar energy. I find that solar energy is best for chakras in the lower part of the body while lunar energy tends to work well for the upper parts. You can also pull deep green energy up from the soil of the Earth itself. This is a great idea if you have a chakra that tends to make wild swings from being depleted to being too hyperactive. Earth energy is grounding and can help anchor the balance of the chakra in place.

Misaligned

A misaligned chakra can feel similar to an unbalanced one. The difference is that a misaligned chakra might not have any particular energy problems, but it could be out of its socket, so to speak. The different parts of the human energy bodies are very mobile, and that's great. The energy mobility of our bodies allows us to be resilient and have different types of experiences. But sometimes the energies get stuck along the way, for whatever reason, leaving us feeling out of place. Have you ever had a day where you just felt generally 'off' with no explanation? It might be the type of day where things just aren't going right, not because of a lack of energy, but because of a lack of direction. That's a good indication that you might need to do some work aligning the chakras.

You can also sense a misaligned chakra energetically, using the same method employed to figure out which chakras were unbalanced. Once you've found the misaligned spot, use your hand to energetically 'push' it into the spot on the body where the chakra is associated. For example, if you sense that the center of your throat chakra is a little too high up into the face and head, gently push it down into the middle of the throat itself. It's important to do this slowly and breathe as you do. Again, allow the body to speak to you. If it's only moving it just a little bit, then that may just be enough for that session and you can try again later in the day. It may take several sessions of doing this to get it back in line if it's particularly misaligned. On occasion I will encounter someone who will have to see me five times or more to get the chakra back in its proper place.

Having your chakras aligned can be a very interesting experience energetically. Many people report feeling big surges of energy followed by a more restful sleep at night. And who doesn't want more energy and better sleep?

Blocked

When a chakra is actually blocked, it's in its most dire state. The problem with diagnosing all chakra issues as 'blocked' is that most people don't often encounter totally blocked chakras all the time. A chakra becomes blocked when it's been so drastically devoid of energy and balance that it's gone into total self-preservation mode, almost to the point of hibernation. This would be like the bodily equivalent of kidney failure. Blocked chakras often don't feel that dramatic on the body, but they can take their toll over time. For example, someone with a blocked heart chakra might not always notice it in their day-to-day activities, but when it comes time to make a big emotional commitment, they'd feel totally locked in place, unable to move forward.

The best course of treatment for a blocked chakra is to open it slowly at first. This can be as simply as taking a few minutes out of the day every morning to imagine bright light flowing from your hands and into the chakra's area, feeling the swirling wheel of the chakra opening like a door. It's important to not force this because the whole process can feel shocking to the system. Instead, go at a steady pace and work on it continuously. Of course, you should also be mindful of the life conditions that have caused it to be blocked in the first place. In our example of a blocked heart chakra, trying simple things like giving a hug or saying 'I love you' to someone you care about is the best way to get to the core of the problem. Healthy chakras rely on healthy daily decisions and conditions that affect their health.

The more you work on opening the chakra, the more vital life energy you can instill within it. Think of it like exercising to increase muscle mass. You wouldn't want to start a weight training routine by deadlifting 100 pounds at once. Start slowly so the body has time to adjust and get stronger.

Exercise: Blessing the Wheels of Light, a Rite for Chakra Clearing and Alignment

This ritual incorporates elements of chakric clearing, balancing, and alignment. It's a good catch-all if you're not sure what's wrong with the chakras and want to do a good 'reset' of the system. It works first by clearing and liberating any trapped energies. Then, new vital energy is pulled in to bring the energy bodies power and closure. This is written as if performed on your own self, but it can be easily adapted to work on another person as well. It can be helpful if you've already become aware of any problem areas in your chakras, although it's not required. This working will begin to take care of most disturbances.

Materials:
Bowl of water
Salt
White votive candle

Begin by laying either flat on your back, or sitting upright with your legs crossed. Breathing slowly and deeply, settle in to your body and become aware of the state of your energy right now, physically and spiritually. Are you tired? Anxious? Depressed? Hyperactive? With each breath, simply observe where you're at right now and make a little mental note of how you feel.

When you feel ready, bring the bowl of water and salt close to you. Focus on the water and touch it with your fingers. Begin to imagine it being filled with bright, white light. Do the same for the salt, allowing them both to fill up with light until you feel it can't possibly hold any more.

Take several pinches of salt and sprinkle it into the water saying:

Oh creature of water, I do bless and consecrate you in the name of life, light, love, and truth.

May you be a vehicle for purification for this my sacred body.
Dip your fingers into the water and dab it onto each of the bodily points of the chakras. As the water touches your skin, imagine the area bursting into a swirling tornado of white light. The blessed water you've made is clearing away anything that is not sacred and perfect. Do this for every chakra and then rub generous amounts of extra water all over the rest of your body. Remember to maintain regular mindful breathing as you do this. Mindful breathing helps to purify the body of any damaging experiences you might be holding onto.

Next, take up the candle and light the wick. Stare into the flames and allow your full attention to flow into it. Focus on the flame and everything it represents to you. Feel the warmth of it on your skin. Feel comforted by everything it's lending you in the moment. Bless the flame saying:

Oh creature of fire, I do bless and consecrate you in the name of life, light, love and truth. May your warmth fill every void and bring this sacred body to fullness and balance.

Very carefully, bring the candle up to each of the bodily points of the chakras. As your skin feels the warmth in each point, imagine that the fire itself is flowing into the chakra and mixing in with the natural swirling pattern of the chakra's own movement. Some chakras might need more of this flame energy than others, so just pay attention to your intuition and what the body is telling you. Also, don't set your hair on fire!

With every chakra purified and empowered, then align yourself to the powers of above and below. This part of the rite helps to keep the axis of the chakras aligned and anchored into place. Our bodies naturally align with the forces of the earth and the heavens above us, so your body will find this to be a very natural and comforting process.

Tilt your head up to the sky and imagine a beam of light

slowly descending from above. As the beam drops over before it reaches your body, the point of it becomes sharper and more focused. Allow the beam to enter into the crown chakra above the top of your head and descend down like a thread. As it does, it enters every chakra on its way down and infuses each one with its light. After it exits the root chakra, see it sinking into the ground like an anchor.

Tilt your head down to the ground and imagine a beam of light arising from the earth. I like to imagine this as a cool, rich, green energy. Just like you did with above, but in reverse, feel the beam move into each of the chakras, starting with the root. Bring the light up until it exits the crown chakra and rises up into the heavens.

Breathe once again, slowly and deeply, and sense how you feel right now. Some people will feel incredibly calm, while others will feel totally jazzed up and buzzing with energy. Anything you feel will be specific to your body and the needs of your energies. This exercise can be performed whenever you like, whether you feel like there's an issue with your chakras or not.

The Aura

Even with no mystical teachings at all, you've still probably heard of the aura. The aura is a part of the energy bodies that extends anywhere from 3 inches to 5 feet (give or take) around the body. If you're looking at the triple-soul model, most people consider the aura to actually be a manifestation of the talker, or middle self. The aura has been depicted in religious art for thousands of years in the form of the halo around or above the head, showing that it's the most 'pure' form of the subtle energy bodies.

Regardless of what you think about what exactly the aura is, there's no doubt that it's important to keep it healthy and clean. Psychics and spiritual seers, even if they disagree on the nature of the aura itself, usually still describe it in similar ways. Many psychics and others sensitive to these things will tell you that people who are sick or tired will have auras that are close to the body and give off dull or dark colors. Healthy and energetic people will show auras that are wide, bright, and filled with bright colors or many types of colors. Of course this is a generalization because the size, shape, and color of an aura will vary dramatically depending on the person and the meanings of their appearance aren't a one-size-fits-all code. This again is where intuition becomes important.

Since the aura can extend far outside the physical body, it's often one of the first things someone will notice about you, whether they're doing so intentionally or not. If you've ever just had a bad impression of someone that had nothing to do with the way they looked or acted, it could have been you sensing their aura. Similarly, there are people who tend to just attract others and seem to bring a whole room together when they come in. Someone 'giving off good vibes' is the influence of their aura touching yours, leaving an impression.

A 'vibe' is actually a vibrational frequency that wafts off the aura like a scent. The reason it's easy for a lot of people to sense one of these frequencies is because they can have a far-ranging influence. Depending on the mood a person is in or how much power they hold onto in that moment, the frequency might be sharper or duller. Really, vibrations like these come in all shapes and sizes, just like the aura itself.

For the purposes of this book, we want to keep our aura and the vibes it gives off fresh and clean. Just as we like to fine-tune our personality to make a good or impactful impression on others, it's in our best interest to do the same for the aura. Another reason why it's important to keep the aura clean is that our vibrations can actually affect other people and other people's vibrations affect us. This explains why you can feel like you're in an excellent mood one moment and in a totally sour mood the next after being around another person (outside obvious reasons like being treated poorly by the person).

Auric clutter is when we encounter vibrations from others that stick onto our own and meld into our own auric fields. Having good protective energies around us is one way to help reduce this, but most of the time it's just something that happen to us, like accruing bacteria on our hands between washings. Too much auric clutter can affect our ability to concentrate, meditate, sleep restfully, and move around within our own energy bodies. Big buildups of auric clutter can even cause issues such as blocked chakras, as we've already discussed.

Consider clearing your aura as part of your regular psychic hygiene, like brushing your teeth. Doing so regularly is a good idea since it's easier to clear away little bits of auric clutter at a time rather than letting it build up and tackling it all at once. It's also very easy to do and I've seen hundreds of creative ways that mystics have found to keep the aura clean. Here's how I do it.

Exercise: Clearing the Aura

Begin by entering a light meditative state however you like. Simply breathing deeply, relaxing all the muscles in your body, and clearing your mind is fine enough.

Once you feel open and receptive to your own personal energy through your meditation, begin to sense the specific aspects and layers of your energy bodies. If it helps, physically reach out and trace your fingers over the points and layers of energy. I like to take a quick scan of my chakras first and then work out from there. The first step in sensing the aura is figuring out how far away from your body it is. As you move your hand further away from your skin, see if you can sense a magnetic push or pull that feels like the edge of something. It might also feel like a buzz or a layer of subtle heat. Remember, the aura can be as close as a few inches from your skin or as far away as several feet. Try to sense the outer edge of your aura without pressure or judgment of what it might mean in that moment.

With a basic realization of where your aura is in the moment, take a moment to once again return to your breathing and focus on the flow of the air entering and exiting your lungs. In your mind's eye, begin to imagine that this air entering you is filled with the same bright, white light that you used to clear the chakras. As you breathe in, imagine the light flowing into all areas of your inner body, including your organs and bones. Continue to breathe this light in and feel your entire body filling up with it until you feel bursting with brilliant fresh energy.

Take your hands against your chest with your palms facing about, like you're about to push something away. Continuing to use the breath to channel the flow of energy, feel the light gathering in your hands and physically begin to push it outwards, to the edge of your auric field. Do this slowly and with intention, being open to any sensations this might bring about.

As the light (and your hands) reaches the edge of where your aura is, sweep your hands up and down like you're washing a surface. You are, in fact, 'washing' the edge of your aura with the light of your breath. Repeat the process of gathering light at your hands and pushing it to the aura's edge, then wiping it clean. Do this until you feel that there's not much left to push out, and that your aura itself has become one with the bright white light of your inner being.

At the end of this I sometimes like to seal up my aura with an intonation. Using tones and sounds is a great way to clear away any residual clutter that might be sticking around. To do this, take a big breath in and sing out the vowel sounds:

eeeeee – aaaaah – oooooh

Clearing the aura can also be combined with the Blessing of the Wheels of Light for a full-on, holistic personal energy cleansing.

Cords and Soul Shards

Throughout our lives we all experience things that are hurtful, agonizing, and downright traumatic. Often this happens through difficult experiences with other people, or situations brought on by difficult people. Sometimes our energy bodies, in an attempt to cope with this trauma, actually develop attachments to the cause of the trauma. In psychology this might lead to codependent behavior, when your personal relationship to someone or something else is actively draining you even when it's not obvious. For a lot of people this codependence simply holds us back from reaching our true potential, which is bad enough. But sometimes it turns into something completely destructive and threatening to our life-force energy. The energy of these disruptive relationships develops something mystical folk call cords. I'll share a personal story to explain more.

When I first started practicing energy work as a teenager, things came pretty easy to me for the most part. I was good at calling and directing energy and using it to improve my environment and my life. But for some reason my relationships with other people (mostly friends) just weren't shifting. Everyone wants better friends regardless of what age you are, but when you're in high school it becomes a very focused priority. I couldn't develop deep friendships with many people in my freshman year and it was really bothering me. This was especially aggravating as I had already done so much work to become the type of person who could attract and develop deep friendships.

When asking my magical teacher for help, she suspected that I might have cords attached to me from the previous trauma of being relentlessly bullied and outcast in middle school. She asked me to go into a meditative state and use my mind's eye to sense any strands of dense energy that might be tugging on any areas of my body.

It took me a couple of tries, but eventually I began to sense a small cluster of dense, dark, strands of energy. If I focused closely, I could actually sense their tugging at my own solar plexus chakra, which was causing me to feel powerless in the situation. After several sessions of meditation and sensing, I 'followed' the strands to their source – memories.

There isn't anything inherently wrong with memories. They are part of our personal history and remind us of who we've become and how we've become who we are. At the end, memories are all we have before we cross into the otherworld at death. I don't want to discount memories or make you afraid of them, but sometimes memories that are burdened with unnecessary trauma just do more harm than good. Traumatic memories are usually what you'll find if you realize that you have cords attached to you.

If you sense and follow a cord and it leads to a vision of something you're not even remotely familiar with, you may have a cord that's still connected to a past life. This sounds outrageous at first. Who would we have cords attached to in a past life? Shouldn't all of that be wiped away when we're born? Well, yes and no. While we do come into this life fresh and ready for new experiences, certain events or traumas can trigger a connection to a traumatic past life experience. These experiences can be so strong that our energy leaks out through our bodies and backwards in time through these cords.

When the energy leaks become constant and powerful, many people believe that you can actually lose fragments or 'shards' of your soul to these past traumas! A big part of many modern shamanic traditions is calling back these soul shards and reclaiming the power that was lost. Look into the practice of shamanic soul retrieval for more on that.

Luckily, cords from past lives and present aren't too difficult to get rid of most of the time.

Exercise: Cutting Cords

If you haven't already, the first step is identifying where your cords are if you have any. This can be tricky unless you're really good at sensing energy. It's important that you not worry yourself over cords to the point of making them up or imagining them. Approach this exercise with wisdom and discernment, trusting your intuition. For this exercise we'll be calling upon the archangel Michael. As long as you can sense your cords, the archangel of the fiery south will do the hard parts.

Materials:
Candle
Knife

While in a meditative state, begin to sense and focus on a cord. If you feel that you have several cords, focus on just one for the purpose of this exercise. You can always go back and finish off the rest.

Use your imagination to follow the cord itself outwards into the invisible world. See it stretching on and on until it lands at a vision of a time and place of origin. This could be something from your current life or something past. Allow the vision to play out before you. This might look like some vague, swirling colors with little meaning, or it could be an entire scene that's clearly visible. Simply observe this without judgment, recognizing it as part of your past, even if it was only days ago. Then release yourself of the vision and allow your consciousness to follow the cord back to your body, knowing that you've given this experience the last bit of attention that it's going to get.

Take up your knife (a special knife specific for energy work is best for this, although any blade will do in a pinch) with one hand and light the wick of the candle in the other. Hover the blade over the flame, close enough to get it hot, but not quite touching the flame itself to the point of burning it.

Imagine that the flame sends a swirling stream of fierce, fiery energy into the blade. See it spiraling around and through the blade, embedding it with the raw power of fire. Do this until you can imagine that the entire blade is a flaming sword.

Lift your flaming energy sword above your head and call out to Michael, archangel of the south:

I call to you Michael, mighty warrior of the south!
Keeper of the flame and the sword of justice, come to me!
All evil cowers before you. All things cruel and foul tremble before
your cosmic presence.

Keeper of time who leads the forces of protection,
aid me in the work of severing all ties that bind.
Assist me in cutting away all that does not serve me.

Michael! I call upon you to cut these cords as I reclaim my sover-
eignty!
I cut these cords in the name of fire and rulership of my own being!

Swiftly bring the blade down and cut away at the cords outside of you, seeing them shatter and burn to a crisp at the touch of the flaming sword. You see the flame of the sword catching onto the furthest reaches of the cord, until it reaches the source and completely vanishes from time and space.

Put the blade down, blow out the candle, and thank archangel Michael with whatever words you like. The archangels are extremely powerful beings and they are always up for helping humanity, but we have to ask them. Michael can assist you with cutting out any negative blocks, whether it is cords or otherwise. We'll talk about him more later in our section on the beings of power. For now, rest and take pride in severing these damaging connections. The rest, as they say, is history.

Baths: Clearing and Uncrossing Washes

Clearing baths are definitely one of my most favorite things about spiritual cleansing. Bathing with some kind of spiritual intent has a history going back for thousands of years. From the bathers of the Ganges River in India to the healing waters of Sulis in the Roman baths, bathing has arguably been the number one most popular method of cleansing since time immemorial.

I first became aware of cleansing baths though my training in witchcraft at an early age, and later on through my studies in hoodoo and other American folk magicks. I remember very clearly when I learned about them because I was admittedly quite a bit skeptical at how it would work. Were these teachings seriously suggesting that to rid myself of negative energy all I had to do was take a bath? Well, yes and no.

The mechanics of spiritual bathing is pretty simple at its core. Water carries a vibration, just like anything else. Clean water picks up not just the regular dirt and grime we accrue throughout the day, but also the psychic debris and auric clutter as well. Since everything in and around us sings with a particular vibration and frequency, it makes sense that the vibration of clean water would work to neutralize unhealthy energy and bring us back to a state of purity.

In hoodoo, there's a strong belief that dirty energy can get tracked into the home by your body in all kinds of ways. It can literally cling to your shoes as you walk and come in with the dirt. It can attach through shaking hands with someone on the street, or being close to others on the subway on the way to work. Even handling the mail, files at work, and books from the library can pose a potential threat. This isn't meant to make you paranoid, but rather to underscore the importance of recognizing that everything we do exposes us to certain energies, for better or worse.

There are so many kinds of spiritual baths that would be impossible to cover and many would fall outside the scope of this book anyway. For that reason, I'll give these two distinct categories of my own: clearing baths and uncrossing baths (also known as uncrossing washes).

The clearing bath is your general go-to bath for most things that stick to your energy bodies. I consider clearing baths to be an umbrella term that covers general cleansing, uncrossing, uncursing, and deconditioning. When you've had a rough day and just need to get the muck off you, a general clearing bath would be a great choice. Even if you're not feeling particularly bad, doing a clearing bath every now and then is just good spiritual hygiene.

Here's a simple formula for one of the most basic clearing baths.

Materials:
Salt
Apple cider vinegar

See, now that's simple! You can even get simpler than that by just using the salt, but the apple cider vinegar adds a little something extra. Salt is the most universal purifying agent and I recommend putting it in any bath you take. Vinegars are an astringent and the vibration they carry is so high pitched it does wonders at stripping off anything that isn't native to your own body. Funny enough, most people know of it for its amazing ability to clean household spaces and getting tough stains and smells out of laundry, as any cat guardian can attest to.

For this simple night-time clearing bath, fill up the tub with water as hot as you can get it. As it is being filled up, pour about ½ cup of salt and ¼ cup of apple cider vinegar. Use your hand to stir up the water and you think about your intention to clear yourself of any unhelpful energies. Imagine that as you stir the water, streams of shining golden light begin to weave through the tub. Do this until you can sense that the entire tub is filled with this bright light.

At this point, many people like to say a prayer relating to

cleansing and purifying that's special to their tradition. If you read more about the hoodoo uncrossing baths in the southern regions of the United States, this is when they'll recite psalms and other prayers from the Bible. If you have a spiritual or religious tradition that speaks to you for this type of work, then feel free to use any verse you like. For a general invocation, you could use these words or similar:

Holy water, sacred well
awaken with the gift of light
Impurities before me quell
as blessed day falls to the night

Step into the tub and immerse yourself underwater fully, seven times in a row. Seven is a holy number and relates to the seven heavenly bodies of the ancients as well as the seven corporeal directions. The act of dunking yourself seven times aligns you with the power of the celestial bodies and calibrates your personal energies to the present moment, leaving all past detachments behind.

Now you can go ahead and soak in the tub for as long as you like. Some people like to sit for a specific period of time, for example seven minutes or one hour etc. Others will just lay down and relax until all of the noticeable tensions leave the body. I like to just soak until I'm nice and relaxed. If I've had a particularly rough day I might also light up the bathroom with candles and play some relaxing music. Sometimes I'll even sit in the tub and pray for my next steps, if a situation calls for it.

Uncrossing Baths and Washes

When I talk about something or someone being 'crossed', it means that they're in a bound-up energetic situation. The common conditions you might be familiar with are being hexed or cursed. I consider a hex or a curse to be an intentional situation that's thrown at you by someone else who knows what they're doing. I think that tends to be fairly rare and it's important to not walk around every day with the fear that someone's hexing you. That attitude just isn't healthy and could do more damage than a hex itself. But it can happen on occasion.

Being crossed is a general condition that results from energy being so damaged or tangled up that your whole system is just blanketed with a feeling of misfortune. Based on this definition you might say that having all of your chakras blocked could be a form of being crossed. You could also be crossed by someone without them even intending to do it to you. Extreme jealousy or hatred by someone else can cause bundles of negative energy to come hurling towards you when they think about or look at you. Hopefully, your general personal protections would be enough to deflect this most of the time, but sometimes they are not.

If you're open to your own psychic senses, you can 'tune in' to your energy bodies and sense if you're experiencing a crossed condition. It might look like the currents of energy that run through your body are tangled up or disjointed. You might also 'see' a film of dark energy covering you in layers. If you're not so open in the psychic sense, you can often tell by more mundane measures. Those days where nothing seems to be going right for you is one indication. Those days lasting in a string of several days or weeks would point to a need to draw an uncrossing bath right away. Even if you're not feeling anything particularly lasting and toxic, sometimes it's just good to do an uncrossing bath now and again to strip off anything that might be lingering outside of your regular clearing baths.

The uncrossing bath focuses not only on conditions you have created for yourself, but also the conditions that other people have thrown at you, whether they knew what they were doing or not. You'll see that what I'm calling an 'uncrossing bath' for the purposes of this book is very similar to what I'm calling the general 'clearing bath', but with a little more oomph and focus on stripping away outside forces.

Materials:
Two white candles
Incense of your choosing
Salt
Apple cider vinegar
One or two of any of the following herbs in leaf, tea, or oil form: Angelica, basil, burdock, dill, hyssop, mint, nettle, oak, patchouli, rosemary, rue, tobacco

First, light up your incense and carry it around the bathroom to clear out any energies that may be lingering in there. For this, we're going to make sure that all energies are as tidy as they can be. If you can't burn incense where you're taking the bath (like in a hotel room, college dorm, etc.) wash as many surfaces of the bathroom as you can with a mixture of hot water and apple cider vinegar. This will not only neutralize any energies in the room, but the mix is great for cleansing those surfaces, too!

As for the herbs, you'll want to prepare those now. If the herb is in liquid form like a tea or oil, then you don't need to do anything else. But if it's dry or fresh, make an infusion out of the herb by steeping it in boiling water for a couple of minutes, like you would with an herbal tea. This is because you are going to be pouring it directly into the bath and you don't want to get your drains all clogged up.

Next, set up your two white candles on the ledge of the tub on the left and right side, so that when you step into the tub you'll have to pass between the two, like a gateway.

With everything set up and prepared, you can fill up the tub. For this part, do the same thing you did with the general clearing bath. Make the water as hot as you can stand it while pouring in the salt and vinegar. See the tub fill with light as you swirl every-thing together.

Once the salt and vinegar are mixed in, you can pour the herbs into the water. The herbs I listed are some of the favorites for uncrossing baths, but there are many other herbs that fall into this category. The books I list in the recommended reading section are good sources for more information about cleansing, clearing, and uncrossing herbs.

Now that the bath itself is ready, it's time to prepare to step into the tub. Hold your hands over the white candles and bless them as they create the doorway, which leaves all anxieties, fears, and expectations of the day behind. As you light the wicks, say:

It is not these wicks that shine bright with flame
But the pillars of the gateways of Heaven.
May this day mark the passage from darkness to light
As I step forth into the waters of purity.
Oh brilliant universe! Lend your power to this rite
As I return to my most perfect, holy state.
The door is open as I greet the waters with courage.
The door is open as the flames kiss the water's edge.
The door is open as I step into the warm embrace of eternity.
Blessed be!

Imagine that the flames rise up; imagine that a brilliant shining gateway is arching over the ledge of the tub, inviting you in. Slowly pass through the gate into the tub. Standing in the tub, immerse yourself in the water thirteen times in a row. Thirteen is a powerful number, relating to the number of moons in a year, the count of months in traditional initiatory cycles, and in numerology – the number of raw power.

Soak in the tub and feel this magickal water penetrating every pore in your skin, flowing into the core of your very being. Its light fills up every void and transmutes anything unhelpful, dangerous, or draining from all energy bodies. Fill your mind with thoughts of peace, achievement, victory, and pride. Pray for purity and peace as the water strips away everything that does not serve your highest good.

When you're done, imagine the shining archway once again and slowly step through it. Blow out each candle, imagining that the archway fades back into the wicks. This is where I say a few words of thanks to the powers for helping me.

If you suspect that something truly dangerous is afoot, like an intentional curse or hex, you may want to repeat the uncrossing path on several consecutive nights. Traditionally, if an uncrossing bath is to be repeated it would be done in any count of three: three nights, six nights, nine nights, and thirteen nights. I would consider a thirteenth night as the 'big guns' work that I'd save for the most dire of situations. But really, you can't cleanse too often so feel free to perform this as long as you feel you need to.

Considerations for the Clearing Bath

When planning a clearing or uncrossing bath, you may want to keep these other points in mind:

Timing: Traditional lore will often say that the clearing bath should be performed before sunrise. The idea here is that you're clearing everything away and starting fresh before you start the day or before you even speak to anyone. If you can manage that, great! The effort of doing something like this before sunrise would certainly add a boost of power to the working and your connection with it. Although this is ideal, life doesn't always allow for such auspicious timing. Parents may not even dream of having this type of time before sunrise. That's okay. Just do what you can and do it with intention.

Pre-wash: Some sources on cleansing baths will say that you should wash off physical grime before you take the bath. Others will say that the cleansing bath will take care of both. If you want to wash off before you bath, I'd recommend a quick scrub down in the shower before moving on to the preparation for the bath.

Herbs and oils: Make sure you don't have any bodily sensitivities to the herbs you're using. Apply a small test patch of any oils on the inside of your arm and watch for any reaction. When using essential oils in the bathtub, just a few drops will do.

Once the bath is done and the water is drained, make sure the tub is cleaned so you're not leaving behind any residual energies for your next bath or shower.

Bath Recipes

Now that you know how to perform a general clearing and uncrossing bath, you can experiment with designing different types of baths for different purposes. If you have specific conditions that you know you're having issues with, custom bath recipes can help target the issue and get right to the heart of the matter.

Most of these recipes rely on specific combinations of oils and herbal infusions. If the ingredient simply says the name of the plant and how much to use, assume that it's meant to be an infusion, or a 'tea' of the plant matter. For example, if you're using a cup of salt for this first recipe, then you'll want to use a quarter-cup for the rest of the ingredients listed. Many of these can be mixed and matched since certain types of plants have energies that span across many functions. Learn more about plants and oils if you want to become your own master of the clearing bath.

Abundance Bath

This recipe focuses on clearing away poverty and want and leaves you feeling ready for blessings to fill up your life. If you find that you're always in the mindset of lacking something, the abundance bath can help.

Materials:
1 part salt
¼ part chamomile
¼ part parsley
¼ part thyme
3 drops patchouli oil

Aura Clearing Bath

This bath would go great with the exercise to clear the aura, although either would most likely have a similar effect. Angelica is the herb of the celestial bodies and your higher nature, so it clears the way for your most pure self to shine though.

Materials:
1 part salt
2 parts angelica

Bravery Bath

Sometimes we just need the guts to make something happen and, for whatever reason, lock up in fear that hold us in place. This bath uses herbs known for infusing courage into the energy bodies and tossing cowardice to the side.

Materials:
1 part salt
⅓ part fig
⅓ part thyme
⅓ part linden flower

Change Bath

Have you ever felt stuck at a certain point in life, knowing that you would have the courage to move forward if only you knew how? This bath works to shake up stagnant energy and get things moving. The way that they move is up to you and the decisions you make after the bath is complete.

Materials:
1 part salt
1 part catnip
½ part basil

Depression Ease Bath

If you're experiencing depression, you need to consult a qualified physician and get help beyond consulting the mystical forces. But if you're doing that already or plan to, this bath can help ease the mental burden a bit and open the way for relief.

Materials:
2 parts salt
1 part sunflower petals
½ part nettle leaf
½ part yarrow
½ part vervain
5 drops lavender oil
3 drops orange oil

Exorcism Bath

No, this isn't the type of exorcism meant to expel the demons of the abyss from a body. Rather, this bath can be used if you feel as though someone else's influence has crept into your being and you now wish to detach from the influence and reclaim your power. This is a good bath for people struggling with codependency or the feeling of being controlled by another person.

Materials:

1 part salt

½ part apple cider vinegar

⅓ part rue

⅓ part vervain

⅓ part daffodil

Healing Bath

Again, you should always consult a physician for illness of the body or mind. This bath can help to zone in on the energy that's attached to illness and disease and drive it out, making way for healing energy to flow.

Materials:

1 part salt

⅕ part agrimony

⅕ part comfrey

⅕ part ginger

⅕ part horehound

⅕ part juniper

⅕ part rosemary

Inspiration Bath

Now here's a bath I love to use! If you've ever suffered from writer's block or the drying out of your creative well in any way, then you can relate to the value of this bath. This recipe shatters blocks that keep the creative juices flowing.

Materials:

1 part salt

1 part bay leaves

½ part jasmine

⅓ part pomegranate juice

Love Bath

The herbs and stones of love clear away lower vibrational energy and open up the heart chakra to both give and receive love. To both move away from heartbreak and open up to love anew, try alternating between this bath and the depression ease bath.

Materials:

1 part salt
1 part rose petals
½ part clover
½ part lavender (or 3 drops lavender oil)
½ part lemon grass
1 sprig saffron
1 rose quartz crystal

Psychic Attack Bath

Although rare, there's little worse than feeling like your mind is being violated by a psychic offender. Psychic attacks can occur even if the attacker doesn't really know what's going on. Sometimes the hateful dreams of someone who detests you can be enough to trigger a psychic attack of some kind. This bath will sever any psychic connections between you and another person.

Materials:

1 part salt
1 part apple cider vinegar
½ part agrimony
½ part rue

Willpower Bath

This bath can help if you feel like you need to strengthen your will to move to forward or solidify your commitment to something. If extreme avoidance is the issue, try alternating between this bath and the bravery bath each night.

Materials:
1 part salt
1 part dill
3 drops frankincense oil (or a couple pinches of the resin)

Cleansing by Heat and Sweat: The Sweat Lodge

I desperately wanted to tell you all a little about sweat lodges, until I realized that I had never actually been to one that affected me in any moving way. Luckily, I found someone who experienced a sweat as a guest and lived to tell the tale! The following is an entry from Jessica D. Rzeszewski, author of *Carry the Rock: An Apprentice Journey.*

A sweat lodge is a time-honored ceremony to cleanse yourself of nearly anything that plagues you. The purpose is to heal via the physical body. Except that I didn't know that when I attended my first sweat lodge.

What I did know was that my new boss spoke in passionate terms about attending a Lakota sweat ceremony in the hills a few hours away from where we both lived and I immediately wanted to attend.

As the time approached for the event, my boss informed me that she wasn't able to go due to a change in her schedule. Did I want to drive out to the location of the sweat and attend by myself? She would be happy to inform her friends that I would be coming. They'd look out for me and assist me during the ceremony.

Yes! I didn't hesitate and the following Saturday, I was careful to follow the directions to the lodge (pre-GPS devices) scribbled on a piece of paper as I drove east into the hills towards Riverside, California.

What was I getting myself into? I was nervous as I made the two-hour drive. I knew little about the Lakota tradition of sweating inside an inipi or womb-like structure heated with stones called 'Grandfathers'. I was curious though.

Recently divorced from my husband of twenty years, I was a new psychotherapist fresh from a graduate program. My job as the therapist to a group of adolescents in a residential treatment program was to practice the theory of 'talk therapy'. However, in my short stint as a therapist, talk therapy didn't appear as effective as I thought it needed to be to assist these young people.

Let me emphasize, in the telling of the experience here, that despite not knowing much about the Lakota tradition, in the end, cleansing took place that impacted my life immensely. Without understanding or thorough knowledge of the sacredness or spiritual nature of the experience, in the end, I was profoundly transformed.

Cleansing is like that: it comes about because the participant intends for healing to take place and inside of that intent is the will and the power to manifest the healing. Whether cleansing takes place via speech or via the body isn't the sole criteria for healing to occur.

Often healing takes place outside of language, just as it did for me, on the level of the body.

Participants were invited to crawl into the lodge and seat themselves around a small pit. Once seated inside, the ceremony commenced. Those outside the lodge would transport stones from amidst a red-hot fire into the lodge in a series of four rounds.

Once inside the pit the stones were sprinkled with water and the resultant steam would saturate those seated in the pitch black of the lodge itself.

Asking if the lodge was hot is like asking if it hurts to get a tattoo. You bet it's hot! You bet that needle hurts tender skin! But the greatest significance is the results. I never anticipated the power in those stones!

Picture in your mind: Participants are seated on the ground with legs crossed. Inside the inipi it is pitch black. Unbearable heat crawls over your skin as the steam from the stones are sprinkled with water. You are dripping from sweat by the end of the first round. When the round ends, the canvas 'door' is opened and the cool of the evening rushes over your feverish face.

The sweat lodge leader asks that you direct your focus onto what you want to let go, what you want to cleanse from your body, what toxins need to seep from the pores of your skin as perspiration trickles endlessly down your nose.

He instructs you to pay attention to the images that arise within your mind's eye. They will inform you as to what needs cleansing.

Suddenly, images of my mother appeared. My mother! She was not the best of maternal figures. She was capricious, cruel with her words, and lacked empathy. Suddenly, I was full of childhood connections that only a daughter can have, except that my memories were painful and filled with shame.

I squirmed. I looked in the darkness for those seated next to me. Were they agonized, as I was? Lifting the small stem of sage to my nose, I breathed through it. 'The sage will cool you if the heat becomes too hot,' the sweat leader had said. Tears rolled down my eyes mixing with the sweat from my brow.

'Pay attention to what the stones are saying to you. Don't allow distraction to cross your path. This is your journey, and no one else can take it for you.' The words of the sweat leader came back to me.

Ah! This is what he'd meant in my sudden interest in those seated next to me. I focused onto the darkness, not the darkness of the inipi, but the darkness within me. The darkness of a relationship that had been hurtful and damaging to a young girl's body and spirit so very long ago. I sat still as a statue and cried silently.

Time disappeared. The singing from the first two rounds was over. We were in the third round, the shortest, but most intense round of the ceremony. Inside the inipi it was quiet. In the extreme heat of the lodge, I sweat from my body and soul those images that held me captive to my mother's negativity and the squelching of my spirit. I let 'her' go from a memory full of excruciating experiences. My body released 'her' in an abundance of tears.

Sweating profusely, I allowed the heat, the stones, the songs, and the fire to cleanse what no amount of talking had been able to. Cleansing and healing became entwined, especially where pure intent, the mind, and body joined together inside the very practical, but sacred, Lakota Inipi ceremony.

The Mystic Follows the Mundane

Everything that changes in the otherworld or the astral world causes change here in the physical or 'mundane' world. This is especially the case when we're talking about energies that affect our own bodies. This is why throughout this chapter I made sure to prescribe worldly changes while pursuing your mystical goals.

For example, eating junk food to the point of getting sick won't be solved by taking a healing bath, although it might temporarily make you feel better in the moment. The obvious answer would be to not have eaten in that way to begin with. But we all make mistakes and in this case, I'd take an antacid first and then go to bed. While in bed I might perform a visualization exercise to expel the pain from my body while I wait for my digestive system to sort everything else out. Using magickal energy in tandem with physical effort is the best way to create any kind of change.

As you move forward with your cleansing and clearing work, remember that the body is connected to so many influences that exist both in the world we can see and the world we cannot. Both are necessary to pay attention to for optimal energetic health and happiness.

Chapter 3

Let's Clean House!

If home is where the heart is, then it must be very important to keep it nice and clean. Most of us realize the importance of keeping our living spaces physically clean. When our spaces are clean, it makes us feel a little calmer, less stressed, and less overwhelmed with the day. If you've ever completed a big project in your home like clearing out the garage, organizing the basement, or even putting away all of your boxes after a big move, you've felt the shift in energy that the physical act of cleaning brings. You feel accomplished, ready to take on the next big thing (or a bunch of small things). Imagine what it would feel like if you kept your home clean physically and spiritually, all at the same time!

The Importance of Home

I cannot stress enough how important it is to maintain a healthy, happy home. It affects everything else in your life, including your ability to communicate with other people outside the home. In ancient Greece, everything outside of the home was considered spiritually dangerous. Since the home is the center of your family's power and abundance, it was considered a major vulnerability to travel outside of it. Keeping up the home with not only physical maintenance, but also spiritual purity, was of utmost importance. If you even left the home at all, devotional offerings were made to the gods to ensure a safe journey.

Although a lot of things may have changed since ancient Greece, the dangers of leaving home are still there. So when you finally get back to your home after a long day at the office or a two-day vacation, it's very important that you step back into a sanctuary. The frequencies of your energy bodies need rest and assurance to regenerate and keep you strong. One of the ways they do that is by taking refuge in safe spaces. And there is no place that should be safer than the home.

When thinking about the spiritual health of the home, there are several aspects of wellbeing to take into consideration:

- Wellbeing of the residents/family
- Physical cleanliness and tidiness of the space
- Whether things are organized or scattered about
- Companion animals living with you
- The layout, colors, and design of the home
- Maintenance of spiritual and physical cleansing procedures

Obviously, the wellbeing of the family is the most important thing. If someone is suffering in the home, there's only so much of that you can cleanse out of the home. That's why before I perform a thorough cleansing of my home, I make sure that those I live with are cleansed first. Physically this could mean that any grievances are aired and a path to communication is open. Spiritually it could mean smudging or purifying residents of the home. These don't always have to be performed in order, but the general formula works well for many.

I've said it before and I'll say it again – the spiritual follows the worldly. Physical cleanliness is a must before embarking on mystical cleansing measures. That doesn't mean your home has to be absolutely spotless all the time (and for families with children, that won't be possible until college). It means that you've made your best effort in tidying up, doing those dishes, and sweeping the dirt off the floor before picking up that smudge stick. The same rule applies to disorganization. If your things are so scattered, then it's going to follow that your mental state isn't going to be all that organized either. Disorganization is a breeding ground for negative energy to collect and accumulate.

Another consideration is the presence of companion animals. Cats and dogs are especially tuned in to energetic currents so it's important to keep them healthy and happy. Keep an eye on the behavior of animals in their home and you can have a built-in detection system for when something isn't right. Just as your dog might bark at the presence of a stranger at the door, he might become aloof or erratic by the presence of chaotic or unhelpful energies in the home. If your cat is usually a lazy lump and all of a sudden seems extra curious or skittish, it might indicate that the time is right for a home cleansing of some kind.

The layout and style of the home can also contribute to the wellbeing of the home and affect how frequently you need to cleanse it. The importance of style and layout is so often debated, even among philosophies such as Feng Shui, which are Chinese principles that help you to pull in the most optimal energies in the home based on how things are arranged and where they're placed.

The final main factor that contributes to the spiritual health of the home is the frequency with which you perform not only physical cleanings, but your mystical ones as well. Some people like to have a cleansing calendar where regular minor cleansing occurs to maintain the wellbeing of the home continuously. Others don't cleanse their space very regularly but instead pick a few special days a year to perform major cleansing and clearing workings. Some do all of that and more! You'll have to determine what the best schedule is for you based on the type of energy that accrues in your home and how fast it gets there.

The Spiritual Anatomy of the Home

Different parts of the home both collect different types of energy and emit different types of energy. Knowing the spiritual anatomy of your home can help a lot when it comes time to perform your cleansing work. The type of cleansing you might perform in the bathroom might be a little different to the type you perform in the bedroom. For example, if you're doing a specific clearing designed to reconnect romantically with your partner, you might not need to focus that working on areas of the house like the garage or basement. Cleansing work designed to clear away blockages in a feuding family might work better if performed in the common areas (kitchen, living room, etc.) rather than the private bedrooms and bathrooms. All mystical work should be performed with intention and a mind for your final outcome. Of course, most of the home cleansing we're talking about here is designed for the whole home in general, and that's great too.

Let's take a look at some of the common energies that rooms in the home can gather and emit:

Living Room

The living room emits earth energy and generally acts as the stabilizer for the whole home. This room tends to gather energy from all over the house, since most residencies have the living room either in the middle of the house, or in a place where you have to walk through it or past it to get to most of the other rooms. I tend to think of the living room as the air traffic control tower for the whole home, so I tend to begin and end my home cleansing workings here.

Kitchen

Some may argue with me about the living room being the energetic center of the home. If they do, then they're going to tell me that it's actually the kitchen. That's a fine assessment too because the kitchen is also extremely important as a nexus of energy for the home. In many cultures around the world, the kitchen is the lifeblood of the home. Being the place where the food is stored and the drinking water flows, it literally contains the elements necessary for our survival as human beings. I associate the kitchen with fire since almost everyone has their oven here, which is a symbol for transformation and sustenance. The kitchen gathers energy that's concerned with keeping the family going. It's important to clean the kitchen regularly, both spiritually and physically, because a lot of the worries of the heads of the house can gather here. All of those concerns about unpaid bills or employment tend to end up here. If I begin my cleansing work in the living room then the kitchen is usually my next stop.

Dining Room

The dining room (if you have one) has a mixture of kitchen and living room energies (and is often placed between or inside the two). If you have a dining room, this should be where the family gathers to eat, even if it's only on special occasions. My family never really ate in the dining room too often, but it was the place where guests would sit, making it a place of communication. The dining room has a mix of earth and fire qualities, which means conflict here can be difficult to cleanse if it occurs often. Family arguments that begin in the dining room tend to return to the dining room.

Bathroom

It probably won't surprise you that I associate the bathroom with water energy. If there is a room in your house that embodies the full meaning of the word 'cleansing' then the bathroom would be it. It's where the cleansing of your physical body takes place, from showers to teeth brushing. It's important to keep bathrooms clean because the energy we cast away in there can linger if we don't cast it out of the bathroom itself. The bathroom should be your cleansing oasis, where you feel confident in ridding yourself of any unwanted influences.

Bedroom

The bedroom is where you dream and where people generally

do a lot of heavy thinking at the end of the day. For this reason, I associate the bedroom with the power of air. If the bathroom is the center of your personal cleansing efforts, then the bedroom is obviously the refuge you return to when you're done. I like to perform bodily cleansing on myself before bed because the protected feeling of being in my bedroom makes it feel like the cleansing working will 'stick' before I have to leave my home and face another day. When cleansing the bedroom, be sure to place special focus on the bed, since so much of our bodily energy resides there because of the amount of time we spend in it.

Closets

I often find that closets become nests for stagnant energy because of how often they're neglected. Disorganized closets usually become the catch-all for things that we don't have any other place for. It's where clothing that doesn't fit us anymore goes to die. It's where we stored away that tool kit that we can never remember when we need it. The simple act of cleaning and organizing a closet emits an enormous amount of positive purification into the home. Anyone who's ever cleaned out a big, messy closet can relate to the sense of accomplishment and peace of mind that comes from having that work done. If your home is generally clean both spiritually and physically yet you sense a lingering stagnation in energy, check all the closets.

Office

If you have an office and actually work in it, then consider it another space for the element of air in the home. It's where you work, think, study, or write. Offices that are created simply because there are too many spare rooms in the house can collect stagnant energy like closets, so keep an eye on that. If you work from home then chances are your office gets used more than many other rooms in the house. Cleansing a busy office space is important because the stress and chaos of work can accumulate in spaces like these. If you work in a home office regularly, try using part of your break time to perform a simply clearing like tossing a splash of holy water here and there in the middle of the day to break up chaotic energy.

Decluttering as a Ritual Act

Even though I just told you that you should take care of physical cleaning and organizing before you get started on mystical practices, you can actually do both at the same time if you have the time for it. Cleaning up and organizing while focusing on the spiritual consequences of what you're doing can feel incredibly empowering and actually help you focus on the work and get it done faster.

As I write this, I moved from my home in the suburbs into the heart of Washington, DC, a couple of weeks ago. The home I was in was huge and I had about three extra rooms all to myself. My currently home is a small one-bedroom apartment, so you can imagine the amount of clearing and decluttering I had to do before moving.

When I took on the task of decluttering my suburban home, I felt so overwhelmed at the amount of things I had accrued over the years. Even though it didn't look like I had a lot of stuff, it seemed that every closet and corner had its own little dark secret stashes of clutter and stored debris that had been left and forgotten. Out of sight, out of mind, right? I knew that the only way I would get up the motivation to take it all on in the time I needed to before the big move was to call in some spiritual help.

Each time I approached a space that needed to be decluttered, I lit a white candle and said a prayer that my work was a ritual act of clearing away the negative connections of the past. Staring at the flame, I made an affirmation that every single thing I threw away or tossed in the giveaway pile was an act of detachment from any unhelpful energies that may have gathered over the years living there. I didn't do this for every space I cleaned, so I did notice that the times I performed this little ritual showed much larger progress and far less time. Your mystical efforts can work alongside your physical goals in most cases if you just remember to get a little creative.

Exercise: Spell to Tackle a Big Mess

This little working is an expanded version of the white candle blessing. Use this spell when you know you have a huge mess, decluttering, or organizational project to take on.

Materials:
White pillar candle
Holy water
Basil (dried)

If you don't already have holy water prepared, go ahead and make some now. Rub the holy water all along the outside of the candle until it's practically dripping. Then roll the candle in as much of the dried basil as you can. Not a lot will stick to the water-soaked candle, but that's okay, we only need a little. Basil is a great herb to purify the home and begin healing processes and the white candle will help you to clean the slate and start anew.

Hold the dressed candle in your hands and imagine streams of light flowing into the candle until it becomes bright and shining in your hands. Bless the candle by saying:

Blessed candle white as snow
holy dew upon the day
Let my motivations grow
And find a path to clear the way.
Blessed be.

Light the candle and place it someplace safe in the general area where your project is. The reason I suggest using a pillar is so you can extinguish the candle and relight it if you need to walk away from the project and continue it on another day. This can be repeated as often as you need to.

Smudging and Suffumigation

A lot of mystically inclined people know what smudging and smudge sticks are. Smudging is the act of bundling one or more dried herbs together (usually white sage) and burning the bundle for purification. Although you can smudge any person, place, or thing, I'm putting this in the home section since that's where you'll most often see this working done.

Before we get into the specifics of the smudge stick, I want to take a moment to explain its origins. The burning of herbs to cleanse an environment or person can be found in cultures all over the world for many thousands of years. Curiously, 'smudging' isn't even a word recognized by most Native and indigenous people in North America, which is the culture most people identify it with. Even more confusing is the fact that many of the common herbs used in smudging (mostly white sage) are actually forbidden to burn or taboo in some tribal communities. I like to use the term 'smudge' because it's easy to say and many people know what I'm talking about when I say it, but it's important to realize that by burning a bundle of sage, you're not tapping into a specific Native American practice by word and verse.

Suffumigation is a more apt word to describe any act of burning herbs, roots, and wood for purification purposes. My older Pagan friends tell me that suffumigation was a more common word to use until the 1990s when 'smudging' became the word of choice. I tend to use the words interchangeably.

In any case, smudging is one of my all-time most favorite methods to cleanse myself and the space around me. It's easy to do and the actual practice makes you feel like you're participating in something very old and holy. Thousands of years before the birth of Jesus of Nazareth, herbs were being burned in temples from Egypt to Tibet and back again. That feeling of doing something old and holy is certainly justified in that sense.

Here are some of the common plants burned for suffumigation:

Benzoin: A resin from species of trees in the genus Styrax, benzoin. A wonderful resin to burn for working with the astral realms, benzoin is good to burn when you're working on clearing an entity from a space.

Cedar: Burning cedar has a lovely uplifting effect on the space around you. I like to burn cedar when the mood in the home seems low or if someone is arguing. Cedar is also widely known as a powerful spiritual healing agent when burned.

Copal: Another resin, copal specifically works to heighten the vibration of a room during a cleansing. Copal makes a great cleansing incense for matters of the heart and communication.

Dragon's Blood: This fiery red resin smells amazing and is burned in cleansing rites to add power and strength to anything you're doing. Burn dragon's blood resin when you need a little more 'oomph' in your working.

Frankincense and Myrrh: Although these are two different resins, I'm putting them together here since they're so often burned together and have very similar powers. Both frankincense and myrrh call in the divine powers to purify a space, which is why it's always been a popular incense mixture to burn in temples. Catholic churches around the world still burn it to this day.

Sage: A favorite for many, sage is a great 'all purpose' herb for cleansing and is easily available to most.

Sandalwood: Sandalwood has transformative qualities that have the ability to take unhelpful energy and turn it into something good. I like to burn sandalwood after other herbs to replace cast-out energy with positive vibrations.

Exercise: Performing a Suffumigation/Smudging Ceremony

If you're using a smudge stick or incense blend that's been pre-made, then you're all set to skip this paragraph and move on. If not, you'll need to bring your plant matter together now. If making a smudge stick, wrap the strands of dried herbs up with twine, tight enough so they don't slip out, but not too tight to the point of not allowing some air to flow through the herbs to catch flame. If using loose herbs or resin, make sure they're placed in a fire-resistant bowl. Even thick stone bowls can get hot so take note of this for your own comfort. I prefer to suffumigate using a cauldron with a metal handle.

If possible, bring everything into the center of the house or the living room. We'll start at the heart of the home and spiral outwards in a counterclockwise direction. Counterclockwise directions turn away energies so that's the direction we'll go in most of the time for most cleansing work. Obviously most houses aren't circular so just do the best you can with that.

Enter a meditative state in any way you choose. As you do, tune in to the intention to purify your home and all within. Tune in also on the plants or resins before you and think about their properties, scent, and appearance. Breathing slow and deep, place your hands over the bowl and say a prayer to bless and activate the plant matter. I usually say something like this:

Holy powers of [name of plant],

awaken and come alive for the work of purification.
May the sacred smoke of your being cleanse this space
of all things cruel, foul, and fell.
So must it be!

Now you can light your plants or resins. Some plant material is self-igniting and will catch flame and burn with the simple touch of a lighter or match. Others, like resins, need to be burned on an incense charcoal that is lit ahead of time and holds the resins and herbs that are sprinkled on it. Note: this is not the kind of charcoal you cook with, but a specific type used for burning incense.

Take the bowl of smoldering plants and walk to the edges of your home. As you do, waft the smoke with a feather or your hand so it visibly reaches all accessible area. Don't forget spaces like inside the shower, all closets, cabinets, and crawl spaces if you can access them. Ideally, every part of the inside of your home should be touched by the smoke in some way.

If there are multiple levels in your home, start from the bottom and work your way up. Remember to spiral through the house in a counterclockwise direction if you can.

When all parts of the home have been visited, return to your starting place and either snuff out the plant matter or allow it to burn itself out. If you're burning things on an incense coal, simply stop putting more on it.

This final part is important and it's often forgotten: open a window! The sacred smoke has trapped and transmuted the unwanted energy in your space so it's important to give it an exit. If you can, open as many windows as possible, but just one will do the trick. If I've burned so much plant matter that the smoke is very thick, I'll sometimes even use a fan to direct it out quicker.

That's it! Now you know how to perform a simply suffumigation or smudging ritual.

Cleansing with the Elements

Since each room of the home embodies particular elemental energies, it stands to reason that we can use the four classical elements to fine-tune the energies of that space. In many forms of mysticism, the elements of air, fire, water, and earth are seen as a microcosmic image of the larger world. Through the classical elements, we can discover characteristics within things that we can match with our own efforts. Like attracts like.

For example, let's say you wanted to perform a simple cleansing on your bedroom using the element it's associated with – air. Since the bedroom embodies the powers of air, calling in that elemental power will align the room with its home element and anything operating at an unhelpful frequency will simply be tuned out and neutralized. To do this, you might pick up a stick of incense and wave it around the room, focusing on the powers of air and the might of wind to come in and sweep things out like a small cyclone.

Here are some ideas on how to cleanse with each element:

Air: Walk around with a stick of incense and a feather, using the feather to waft the smoke around. You could also take your besom and energetically sweep the floors, ceilings, and walls with it.

Fire: Just like you did with the incense, you could take a small candle and move it around the room so that its light touches all spaces in the room. Imagine the flame leaping out of the wick and swirling around the room, consuming anything that shouldn't be there.

Water: Holy water or any kind of sacred liquid wash can be sprinkled around the room or even cleaned with it. If you want to get very detailed, you could wet a rag with the holy water and wipe down all the surfaces of the room that you'd normally clean.

Earth: Sprinkle salt in the corners of the room in small amounts to shatter the hold of negative energies. You could also do the same with dried herbs that have cleansing and clearing properties.

Cleansing the room with its native element isn't all you can do with the elemental powers. The elements can and should be used to cleanse just about anything you like. To cleanse an object, try passing it through each of the physical elements starting with incense for air, a candle flame for fire, holy water for water, and finishing by covering it up in a bowl of salt.

Exercise: Rite of the Four Powers – Cleansing Space with the Elements

This ritual uses each of the elements to cleanse any space, including your entire home. I consider this 'big guns' work and usually only do it a couple of times per year.

Materials:
Red candle (or white will do)
Bowl of holy water
Incense
Feather
Bowl of salt

Just like the smudging exercise, have all of your materials in the center of the home if you can. I like to set up a little temporary altar for this, which might also have photos of my family and ancestors along with some special stones of power. This will be 'home base' for the rite.

Light the incense and let the smoke rise up before you for a moment, focusing on the gifts of air. Imagine a gentle, healing breeze flowing through the space as you invoke the power of air by saying:

Spirits of the east, powers of air
gift of the eagle and inspiration
enter this space and purify it with your presence.
Powers of air, hail and welcome!

In a clockwise motion, waft the incense around the home, continuing to focus on the cleansing breezes of air coming to your air for purification. When you're done, bring it back to your central altar space.

Hold the candle and imagine yourself glowing as a burning ember in the cold, a source of light and warmth in the home. Light it and safely hold the flame close enough to feel its radiance as you focus on the gifts of fire. Imagine a swirling candle flame sweeping through the home and filling it with a benevolent warmth with the powers of fire as you say:

Spirits of the south, powers of fire
gift of the lion and passion
enter this space and purify it with your presence.
Powers of fire, hail and welcome!

Again, walk clockwise with your candle in every space that allows the light of the flame to touch and illuminate it. Continue to focus on the powers of fire and the gifts of passion, the cleansing fire of the south. Then return to the central altar.

Take up the bowl of water and imagine yourself standing on the shores of a mighty ocean as the waves crash all around you. Focus on the renewing forces of water as you say:

Spirits of the west, powers of water
gift of the salmon and the mystery of dreams

enter this space and purify it with your presence.
Powers of water, hail and welcome!

Sprinkle the water all around the house. Rub it on the frames of the doors and windows. I also like to anoint the windows themselves with protective symbols and prayers. Don't forget to throw sprinkles of water up to the ceiling as well before returning to the center.

Finally, hold the bowl of salt and image that the space you're in is actually nestled in the side of a tall mountain, within an old-growth forest. It's almost as if you can smell the raw earth and hear the whistles of the animals around you. Focus on the regenerative forces of earth as you say:

Spirits of the north, powers of earth
gift of the stag and stability
enter this space and purify it with your presence.
Powers of earth, hail and welcome!

Sprinkle small bits of salt all around the space. As you do, imagine any unwanted remaining energies shattered and destroyed by the mighty powers of earth. Don't worry about getting the ceiling since the holy water had some salt in it for that.

Once you've returned to the center, stare at the candle of fire, take a few deep breaths, and focus on the powers of the elements flowing through the space, which is now completely purified and refreshed with the elemental focus. Know in all parts of your being that your space is not only cleansed and purified, but also balanced and empowered with the Four Powers.

When you're ready, cup your hands before you as if you were holding some water within them. This is a devotional position that shows praise and thanks. It's important that we show gratitude to the Four Powers, as they always choose whether or not they will even show up. Make a statement of thanks that comes from the heart. I typically say something like this:

I give thanks and praise to the Four Powers!
Air, fire, water, and earth
May there be peace and power in your houses.
If you leave this space for your lovely domains
I leave you with love and bid you hail and farewell!

Floor Washes

Popular and highly common in hoodoo tradition, floor washes are essentially the same as a cleansing bath, except used on the floor and counters. Most of the time the same herbs and ingredients are used, although usually with a physical cleansing agent like a soap.

Lore about floor washes goes back to at least the 19th century in North America, the most basic being water, salt, and some soap. The ingredients are mixed together and prayed over (usually a psalm from the Bible if you're looking at the traditional hoodoo) and then used as mop water.

A specific floor washes product called Chinese Wash has become the gold standard for floor washes within the past one hundred years. It comes prepared and sold with the slogan: 'Wash away that evil mess with Chinese Floor Wash!' You can also make it yourself by mixing a few drops of Van Van oil (lemongrass, citronella, vetiver, gingergrass, and sometimes lemon verbena) with a standard floor cleaner (such as Pine-Sol) into your mop water.

Besides Chinese Wash, you can make a floor wash using the same ingredients as the cleansing bath in the earlier chapter. The general rule is that you should use a basic clearing type of wash and then later (or after in the same day) use one of the specific washes designed to draw something in like love, money, luck, etc. With washes, you'll want to start at the top of the house and work your way down, mopping and wiping in a counterclockwise direction.

Sprays

Making a mystical cleansing spray is a wonderful way to incorporate a simple cleansing practice for the home (or any space) when you can't burn candles or incense. Even when you can, a spray is a great way to literally infuse the very air around you with purifying powers.

The most basic spray is an infusion of hot water and herbs, although I also like to add some sweet-smelling oils to leave a lovely scent in the room. Most of the cleansing herbs we use in the cleansing baths and floor washes can work for sprays, but I tend to avoid adding any vinegars to sprays since I prefer to not have the air smell entirely of vinegar. It's also not fun to get in your eyes. You can also add salt, but be careful to not put too much in a spray because it can crystallize inside parts of the bottle and block the spray nozzle from being able to get the liquid out. For all of those reasons, I prefer to stick with herbal infusions and oil. Here are a few of my favorite spray recipes that are designed to go into a 24 ounce spray bottle. Increase or decrease the amount of water to fit the type of bottle you're using.

For each of these recipes, heat the water to near-boiling and add in the herbs. Strain off the herbs, allow the mixture to cool completely, and pour it into the spray bottle.

Basic Home Cleansing Spray

Materials:
3 cups water
4 sprigs of fresh rosemary or 3 tablespoons of dried herb
Juice from ½ a lemon
Optional: 3 pinches of salt

I chose rosemary and lemon for my basic cleansing spray because both are powerful purification plants while also being incredibly easy to find in any market. The bitter powers of lemon destroy harmful energy and the healing properties of rosemary purify and transmute anything left over.

Although the ingredients of this spray are powerful enough on their own, I always like to charge the final product by holding it in my hands and blessing it. For the basic cleansing spray recipe I like to say:

Waters of the cosmic ocean
rosemary lemon grown by day
awaken to this holy potion
purify and clear the way.
So must it be!

Argument Clearing Spray

Materials:
3 cups water
3 tablespoons dried basil or 5 drops basil oil

This spray is great for feuding families or couples going through a rough patch. Though you should always try to get to the source of a problem, this can help ease tensions and clear the way to open communication.

Nightmare and Insomnia Spray

Materials:
3 cups water
5 drops lavender oil
1 tablespoon dried mint

Regardless of what's keeping you from getting a restful sleep, this spray neutralizes chaotic energy in the room to help set your mind at ease. Spray in the bedroom right before bed. This can also work for kids who are experiencing night terrors. Let them spray it themselves and encourage them to use it as their monster fighting repellent.

Sick Room Spray

Materials:
3 cups water
4 sprigs of fresh rosemary or 3 tablespoons of dried herb
Small splash of pure apple juice

Banishing illness and disease from another is as old as the practice of cleansing in general. Sprays to clear away sickness are especially useful when you're visiting someone in the hospital or nursing home and won't be allowed to burn candles or incense, or if you can't stay with them for long periods of time. Rosemary's purifying powers combined with the healing power of apples is a fabulous combination for clearing the way to health and wholeness.

Mars Spray

Materials:
3 cups water
1 tablespoon cloves
1 clove garlic
3 pinches cayenne pepper

I also call this 'fighting spray' and it's used on rare occasions when you feel like someone is actively seeking to destroy you in whatever way. This stinky spray will completely wipe out any destructive energies from hexes, curses, or negative thoughts that may settle in your home. For added impact, drop a rusty nail into the spray bottle. Be careful that you don't get this in your eyes.

Ars Gaudium Spray

Materials:
3 cups water
Peel from 1 lemon
Peel from 1 orange
Optional: 1 tablespoon hyssop leaf
Optional: 3 drops orange oil

For this spray, there's no need to strain the peels out because they'll continue to leach their lovely oils into the water. I call this spray 'the art of joy' because it's really hard to stay in a bad mood for long with the adoring scents of the citrus plants to uplift the spirits and cast out the darkness.

Moon Spray

Materials:
3 cups moon water
13 small pinches of salt
Optional: 2 tablespoons dried mugwort

For this spray, first make moon water by placing a few cups of water under the full moon for the night in some place where the moon's rays will be directly cast onto the water. Moon spray can be used to untangle complicated situations and allow everyone in the space to 'go with the flow', just as the moon controls the rocking motions of the tides.

Get Thee Behind Me Spray

Materials:
3 cups water
3 tablespoons dried lemon balm
1 pinches dirt from a crossroads
1 teaspoon saltpeter
Optional: 1 tablespoon dried rue

This spray would fall under the category of a 'road opener', which is a formula designed to remove obstacles that block your way. Use Get Thee Behind Me Spray regularly in your home when you feel there are constant obstacles and hindrances getting in the way of your success and wellbeing.

Archangel Michael Spray:

Materials:
3 cups water
3 tablespoons dried angelica root
5 bay leaves

Michael is the archangel of the south, ruling over the powers of fire, courage, battle, and victory over evil. This is a great all-purpose spray to call in help from outside forces, but works particularly well if you wish to clear your home from unhealthy attachments. Michael's flaming sword will sever all that binds you from the true you.

Crystals and Stones

While stones can definitely be used for personal cleansing, I'm putting them in this chapter because there are just so many amazing ways you can use stones to cleanse the home and spaces in general.

Many people think of stones as things that need to be cleansed all the time (which is also true) but not as tools that can do the cleansing. In the spirit of using everything we can to cleanse our lives and reach our goals, I propose we take advantage of the powers of stones and use their gifts whenever we can. And hey, they're usually pretty to keep around.

Let's take a look at some of the crystals and stones commonly used for cleansing, clearing, and purification:

Amber: While not actually a stone, it's usually classified as such because of its natural texture and hardness. Amber transmutes toxic energy in the atmosphere.

Black Tourmaline: Traps crossed conditions and sends them a safe distance away.

Bloodstone: Cleanses the body of physical impurities and the energy of disease and illness.

Calcite (Icelandic): Cleans the energy bodies of impurities.

Chalcedony: A powerful cleanser, this stone sucks in negative energy and dissipates it from existence. A great stone to use with dark and dangerous energy that you don't want to touch.

Citrine: This stone never needs to be cleansed by outside means. It traps negative energies on contact, neutralizes them, and emits them back into the space as a positive force.

Diamond: The frequency of diamonds is so high that lower vibrational frequencies become so uncomfortable they simply vacate the premises. Wearing a diamond while in the home keeps the energy high and ensures that unwelcome energy will be immediately grounded and transmuted.

Garnet: This is a great stone to use when working on clearing the chakras. Lay down and place it on the bodily area of the chakra and the garnet will work to purify it of all energetic toxins.

Jade: Clears away blockages from the heart chakra and opens the way for emotional healing.

Jet: Similar in texture to amber, jet is also not technically a stone. Jet is a witch's stone that works to conduct energy and send it along the proper channels. Keep jet in your home when you want to shake up stagnant energy and keep things moving.

Opal (Green): Cleanses the body of oppressive emotions and works to transmute them into feelings of joy and openness.

Peridot: This powerful cleanser opens up the heart and solar plexus chakras and draws away impurities while instilling useful energy for the future. Peridot can help cleanse an environment from cumbersome connections to past influences.

Pyrite: This stone works to lift up the individual energies of many people who are in the same space. This is a great stone to keep around if you have a big family or need to share space with many other people for any length of time. I find that holding pyrite opens communication in an environment where others are closed to it.

Selenite: This beautiful white crystal is great for detachment and is a great stone to bring into the home when you wish to expel unwanted entities.

Quartz: The ultimate all-purpose stone, quartz cleanses the souls of all impurities and amplifies the holy nature of our inner beings. Different types of quartz perform different types of cleansing. Smokey quartz is great to use when you are in danger from outside influences as it turns dark energy back to the center.

Turquoise: This purifying stone traps physical pollution and transmutes it. This would be a helpful stone to keep in the home if you live in a city or another area where smog and environmental pollutants are a concern.

Stones can provide a great addition to your cleansing practice because of how extraordinarily easy they are to use. The energies of stones and crystals go to work immediately when they're even in the general vicinity of a person or place and just become more effective when they're put to use with intention. For the body, any of the stones above can be used for the descriptions I listed on any chakras that you're struggling to keep healthy. The general go-to method for personal cleansing with a stone is to simply carry it on your person, whether set in jewelry or just put in your pocket for the day. The same sort of thought applies to spaces like the home, but there's so much more we can do with them there.

Crystal Purification Grids

A crystal grid is an arrangement with stones that works to set a specific current of energy in motion within and around it. A quick search online will reveal thousands of arrangements, many of which are dazzling and beautiful to behold. Crystal grids are very popular with mystics within the new age movement and you'll see layouts for them suggested in metaphysical stores around the world.

Most grids take on geometric shapes and tend to be arranged in patterns of stars, circles, squares, or combinations of all of them. Even three stones on their own are all you need to create a grid. Generally, pointed stones are arranged to point outwards on the grid to extend energy outwards in varying directions and stones pointed inwards direct energy to someone or something placed in its center. The points on crystals are like flashing arrows that say 'put the power here.' You'll also find grids that are layered to focus certain energies inwards while projecting some energies outwards.

For the purpose of cleansing the home, I recommend making a grid of concentric squares to mimic the shape of most rooms and homes. To make a basic home cleansing grid, place a cleansing stone listed above in each corner of a room or in each corner of the house or apartment as a whole. For stones to simply deflect negative energy like black tourmaline, you'll want to have each point facing outwards unless they're double-pointed or tumbled. For stones designed to purify and transmute the energy within such as clear quartz, face any points inwards towards the center of the home or room. I find that the stones work together well when I use the same type all around in one layer, and then put different types in different layers. For example, you might put that black tourmaline on the very inner edge of every corner in each corner, and then put your quartz right behind it consistently in every corner.

If you own property and are comfortable with digging up some ground, you can bury stones around the points at the edges of the property boundaries. Since the stones are surrounded by the pure soil of the earth, they're being constantly cleansed and recharged automatically. Even if you can't dig a hole for them, a small enough stone can be inserted into soft soil with the push of a thumb or a sturdy stick.

Exercise: Laying a Deflection and Purification Grid

Materials:
4 of any stone that deflects negative energy
4 of any stone that purifies and transforms energy
Salt
Candle

This exercise is designed to lay and activate a basic cleansing grid that both stops negative energy from entering the space and works to transmute any that happens to get through into energy that's positive or helpful. Think of this grid as a strainer that keeps out anything totally unmanageable and then works to heal and feed the home by transforming energy into a neutral state for the mystic to work with. Determine ahead of time if you're laying the stones in a specific room, in the outer edges of the house, or on the boundary lines of the property.

First, lay all eight stones before you and light your candle. Enter a meditative state that's natural for you and gaze at the candle's reflection. Acknowledge in your mind that the flame of the candle is acting as a generator of power to purify, bless, and charge the stones for your work. The stones carry natural vibrations on their own, but your empowerment of them will add to the strength of the work while simultaneously affirming your specific intention.

Take up your first stone and hold it close enough to the candle that the flame gently heats the surface of the stone. While you do, imagine that a swirling tornado of fiery power flows into the stone, penetrating it to its very core. Do this with all eight stones until they're all buzzing with the fiery power. Now you're ready to lay the stones of the grid.

Take the deflection stones and move to your first point, which should be one of the corners. Approach the corner with the stone and slowly lay it on the ground, imagining as you do that a fiery wall of light springs up in that spot, covering a fourth of the area of the home, room, or property with a wall of protection. Do the same with the other three deflection stones until they're all laid and you perceive four walls of fiery light surrounding your space.

Now take the purification stones and move to a point in the space that is in between two of the deflection stones. Try and make this as even as you can, although it certainly doesn't have to be perfect. Lay the first stone on the ground and imagine a golden, crystalline net rising up in its place. The net sparkles and shines with stars as it rises up to a central point above you, covering a fourth of your space. Lay the rest of the purification stones in between each of the deflection stones until the shining net encircles you around and above like a tent. The crystalline net will trap and transmute all harmful energies that penetrate the fiery wall and disperse only helpful power into the space, feeding the home and the wellbeing of all within.

Finally, take up the salt and walk counterclockwise around the space, sprinkling just a tiny pinch in between every stone. The purifying powers of the salt will seal and link up the power of all eight stones, ensuring they all work in harmony while the grid settles into place for the night. The salt can be swept away the next day, but leave it alone for at least one night. And then you're done!

Feel free to add to the grid with new stones as you like. I recommending removing one layer of stones every few months or so and cleansing them in cold water before returning them to place and reinforcing the candle charge and visualization.

Hekate's Deipnon: A Case Study in Ancient Religious Home Cleansing

Years ago I made a new friend, a Hellenic polytheist living in the United States, and she introduced me to a cleansing practice that changed my life. During a pagan camping festival, Cara taught me about the ancient Greek celebrations of the Deipnon and Noumenia.

The Deipnon, meaning 'evening meal', is part of a monthly three-day event observed in the home by families. The day of the Deipnon was known to the Greeks as being placed on what we would consider the new moon, or when no moon is visible in the night sky right before it begins to wax. Its primary purpose is a meal given to the goddess Hekate in a plea to placate wandering spirits and to ask for her favor in the coming months. As a cleansing rite, it's also designed to rid the house of impurities so it can be ready for the month ahead. This is done through a mixture of offerings to the goddess, ritual cleansing like fumigation, and physically cleaning the home.

With the home cleaned both spiritually and physically, the Noumenia is observed on the next day when the very first sliver of the moon is visible in the sky. Although the ancients would have named this the 'new moon', we would specify to call it a waxing crescent. On the Noumenia, a feast is held for the family in honor of the gods Apollo, Zeus, and Hestia. Offerings are given to ask that the family's cupboards be full for the month and that no misfortune be allowed to befall the home.

At the time I had been experiencing a lot of negative issues in the home that required constant cleansing. After a couple months of doing my standard cleansing work every few days or so, I was simply exhausted. So I decided that on the new moon cycle, I would start incorporating Hekate's Deipnon into my regular practice for a while.

When the day came, I began that morning by cleaning the house top to bottom. The carpets were vacuumed, the floors mopped, the windows washed, the laundry done, and all trash taken out to the curb. I learned from others that while it's not always necessary to make the home look like it's fresh off a buyer's catalog, it is important to make your very best effort in making the space as clean as possible. If it takes you a while to clean due to time constraints, you can even start some days early before the Deipnon to get it all done. In my case, my first Deipnon required about three days of pre-cleansing before the day itself. An hour here, an hour there, and voila!

That night I began to prep for my offerings and prayers to the goddess Hekate. As a devotee of the goddess already, it was easy for me to pour some wine, light some incense, and cut some bread for her and the wandering spirits. If you're not already familiar with Hekate or any of the Greek gods and wish to form a relationship with them, observing the Deipnon and Noumenia each month can be a fabulous way to get started. Even though I felt I already had a good relationship with the crossroads goddess, it was nothing compared to how close we became once my monthly devotions on the Deipnon became regular.

To make an offering to Hekate to purify the home, try pouring out a bottle of red wine (known to be appealing to chthonic deities) directly into the ground while saying one of her hymns. If you live in an apartment building or have no immediate open access to the bare earth, you can pour it into a bowl and then dump it on the ground later. While pouring the wine I usually say a prayer at the same time. Sometimes I say whatever I feel inspired to in the moment and sometimes I'll say one of the classic hymns. One of my favorites was Hesiod's hymn.

Hymn to Hekate from Hesiod's Theogony

Hecate whom Zeus the son of Cronos honored above all. He gave her splendid gifts, to have a share of the earth and the unfruitful sea. She received honor also in starry heaven, and is honored exceedingly by the deathless gods. For to this day, whenever anyone of men on earth offers rich sacrifices and prays for favor according to custom, he calls upon Hecate. Great honor comes full easily to him whose prayers the goddess receives favorably, and she bestows wealth upon him; for the power surely is with her. For as many as were born of Earth and

Ocean amongst all these she has her due portion. The son of Cronos did her no wrong nor took anything away of all that was her portion among the former Titan gods: but she holds, as the division was at the first from the beginning, privilege both in earth, and in heaven, and in sea. Also, because she is an only child, the goddess receives not less honor, but much more still, for Zeus honors her. Whom she will she greatly aids and advances: she sits by worshipful kings in judgement, and in the assembly whom she will is distinguished among the people. And when men arm themselves for the battle that destroys men, then the goddess is at hand to give victory and grant glory readily to whom she will. Good is she also when men contend at the games, for there to the goddess is with them and profits them: and he who by might and strength gets the victory wins the rich prize easily with joy, and brings glory to his parents. And she is good to stand by horsemen, whom she will: and to those whose business is in the grey discomfortable sea, and who pray to Hecate and the loud-crashing Earth-Shaker, easily the glorious goddess gives great catch, and easily she takes it away as soon as seen, if so she will. She is good in the byre with Hermes to increase the stock. The droves of kine and wide herds of goats and flocks of fleecy sheep, if she will, she increases from a few, or makes many to be less. So, then, albeit her mother's only child, she is honored amongst all the deathless gods. And the son of Cronos made her a nurse of the young who after that day saw with their eyes the light of all-seeing Dawn. So from the beginning she is a nurse of the young, and these are her honors.

Another lovely prayer is the Orphic hymn to Hekate:

Lovely Hekate of the roads and crossroads I invoke;
In heaven, on earth, and in the sea, saffron-cloaked,
Tomb spirit, reveling in the souls of the dead,
Daughter of Perses, haunting deserted places, delighting in deer,
Nocturnal, dog-loving, monstrous queen,

Devouring wild beasts, ungirt, of repelling countenance.
You, herder of bulls, queen and mistress of the whole world,
Leader, nymph, mountain-roaming nurturer of youth, maiden,
I beseech you to come to these holy rites,
Ever with joyous heart and ever favoring the oxherd.

With the wine libation poured, I move on to the spiritual purification process. On my first Deipnon I opted to keep things simple by carrying around a smoldering bowl of incense and whispering prayers for purification of our home and any wrongdoings that my family may have committed throughout the month. Over the years this has ended up changing each month depending on what I feel needs to be done. Once you get into the groove of the Deipnon, I recommend any of the home cleansing exercises in this book. If you want to get down to the core of what the Deipnon represents in my opinion, the pleas to Hekate constitute an enormous energetic shift to the energy of the home on its own. The act of humble surrender to the powers that be with a plea for help are ritual acts as old as civilization itself.

Once the offering is given and the home cleansed, make sure you clean up your working area as well as you can and throw away any incense ash or other ritual debris.

On the following night, you can observe the Noumenia by enjoying your clean home with a feast for yourself and (if you have one) your family. This doesn't need to be anything major, but it should feel special somehow. On my first Noumenia I prepared a marvelous feast for my home with multiple dishes and several drink options. Anyone who's ever cooked a large meal knows how much work it can be. Consider the effort an act of devotion to the spirit of the home and to the energy of your family and dwelling. That doesn't mean that you need to prepare a vast quantity of food. Usually I'll keep the meal simple yet meaningful by preparing a dish from scratch, trying out a new recipe, or making the favorite dishes of my partner. And don't forget about your family members who meow, bark, swim, and fly! A few extra treats for companion animals can go a long way, too.

The most important part of the Noumenia is the warm feeling you and any family members get from the night. Try to get in some face time with them by planning a game or anything that can stir up a conversation and bring everyone together. Even renting a new movie and talking about it afterwards can add to the special spirit of the night.

With the home cleansed on the Deipnon and newly blessed on the Noumenia, you're starting off the lunar month with a fresh outlook, a warm glow, and hopefully a joyous attitude for the weeks to come. I know that after just a few months of working the Deipnon and Noumenia into my practice, my home and life began to change. No longer was I constantly trying to keep up with rapid cleansing as an effort to keep life's stressor away. I had established a routine for a healthy home that I still follow to this day, years after I learned it.

The Deipnon and Noumenia practice is a good reminder of why we even bother with spiritual cleansing in the first place. Sometimes the very act of cleaning out the old, making way for the new, and working on those things together brings you more peace and power than the result you get from it.

Chapter 4

Hexed, Crossed, or Cursed

Now that you have a practical foundation of cleansing, clearing, and uncrossing tools at your disposal, let's talk about the conditions made by other people that can cause us to enter a state of imbalance, sometimes to the point of being entirely energetically disabled. Let's talk cursing.

Forget what you've heard in movies and novels about curses. Curses and other negative conditions placed upon you by others can sometimes be worse than you realize or a lot easier to deal with than you realize. In short, no two curses are alike and no two victims are alike. While entire books have been written on curses and how to unravel them, this chapter will focus on some basic identification techniques along with methods of uncursing that complement the foundational exercises from earlier in the book. But first we must look at what curses and hexes are.

The Birth of a Curse

The interesting thing about curses is that most of the time they're unintentional. Most of the intentional curses and hexes you might find online or in nefarious magical texts are incredibly hard to muster up the energy for and even harder to place effectively. This is thanks in large part to our human energy anatomy.

We know from looking at spiritual anatomy that there are multiple layers and parts of the self that outside energy has to get through to have it latch on in any permanent or semi-permanent way. That's the first challenge of the would-be hexer. To truly affect you as a victim in any way that you would notice, it generally needs to pass by your personal spirit guides and any exterior protective layers of energy you've set up around yourself. It must then pass through the outer layer of the etheric body. If it survives penetration of the auric field, it must then latch on to your soul parts or other parts of your energy bodies.

As a tarot and rune reader at a metaphysical store, I have seen countless customers come in and complain about a curse that they're sure was placed upon them intentionally by some enemy or handed down through their own family lineage. Ninety percent of the time what the person thinks of as an intentional curse placed upon them doesn't even exist at all. In the 10 percent of times when it does, it is usually not there because of the specific intent of another to curse. Though, of course, there are always exceptions.

Most of the time what someone thinks is a curse upon them is actually what I would call a 'crossed condition'. This can feel like a curse, but it's actually only the symptoms of what might look like a curse. This is important because crossed conditions are usually of our own making or of the unintentional making of others. A good example of this is the harboring of anger towards another person. Let's say a colleague who is always giving you a hard time and hardly works at all got the promotion that you worked really hard to get. Since there is probably nothing you can do about that, you're likely to harbor pent-up anger at the person. Not unleashing the anger in some way might make you feel like you're being responsible, but you could end up accidentally conjuring up a crossed condition for the person. That pent-up anger will find its way out somehow, usually through your gaze, through something that you touched and gave the person, or even by saying hello to them on the way into the office. Before you know it, your colleague comes down with a flu, becomes depressed, or just has a bad few days in general. You may not have intended to, but you essentially shot a hex their way without even realizing it. And since we tie ourselves to energetic acts placed on others, you're then tied to the crossed condition that you unknowingly placed, which has a good chance of leaking out on you.

This is just an example, but think of all the other ways this could happen. Every day many of us do things that make others angry, jealous, or depressed. I don't point that out to say that you deserve to be unintentionally crossed or that you should be paranoid about having it happen to you, but it can happen and knowing that it's happening is half the battle.

Diagnosing a Curse, Hex, or Crossed Condition

The easiest way to immediately diagnose a curse is to visit a healer, psychic, or seer whom you trust and hold in high regard. It's extremely important to not visit a psychic off the street for this type of advice and diagnosis. While psychism can be a noble and helpful profession for many, there are a lot of scam artists out there who like nothing more than to take advantage of vulnerable people and their money. In the shop where I work as a reader, I am constantly encountering folks who come in saying that a psychic has diagnosed them as being cursed to the point of utter inevitable destruction. Of course this is usually accompanied by the assurance that said psychic can remove the curse for a fee, which I've seen range anywhere from $100 to $10,000. If you have no trusted psychic ally on your side who won't cheat you, then it's best to proceed with your own diagnosis.

First, look for any unusual physical and mental conditions. Sudden mental issues like nightmares, panic attacks, and depression can signal an interference in the energy bodies. Again, this only applies if these conditions are foreign to you. I've noticed that it's generally easier for a curse to affect the mental body before it can affect the physical due to the subtle ways the mental body can shift on its own in a short amount of time. Take note of other unusual mental lapses such as chronic sudden forgetfulness, being confused or easily distracted, or being quick to unusual outbursts of anger.

Physical issues might involve seemingly random aches and pains that vanish as quickly as they appear, general tiredness, physical exhaustion, stomach pains, or skin irritations like pin pricks. In extreme cases it could mean the onset of a cold or flu that lasts a very long time.

Concerning physical and mental diagnosis, it's important to consult a physician if you're experiencing difficulties. Do not think that just because you suspect a curse may be at work that it's unnecessary to seek conventional medical help. Quite the opposite. True victims of curses and crossed conditions who experience physical and mental ailments should be especially roused to seek medical attention while also working on possible spiritual solutions as well. The act of healing on its own can even be enough to break the hold of a curse anyway, without requiring mystical aid.

On the mystical side, there are quite a large number of methods that people have used to detect curses throughout human history. The method I'm going to share with you was taught to me by a past teacher and I've found it to be a highly successful way of not only determining a crossed condition, but also in checking out other ways that my energy bodies might be shifting out of a healthy balance.

Exercise: Curse Detection Meditation

This meditation is similar to the other exercises earlier in this book that look into blocked chakras and cluttered auras. We're going to get a little more specific here and look for specific energetic trends that might indicate that you could be in a curse situation.

Begin by entering a meditative state with whatever method you choose. Focus deeply on the movement of your breath and take as much time as you need to enter the meditative state. It's important to not rush this beginning part of the process since picking up on the subtle energies of a curse requires us to open up fully to our bodies, both physically and spiritually.

When you're ready, begin to examine your energy bodies,

starting with the layers that are furthest away from you. If you're experiencing some kind of crossed condition like a curse or hex that's come from another person, it's very likely that it would be tangled up in these outer layers. Remember, it's generally quite difficult for a foreign curse to penetrate these outer layers. If you pick up on something in the outer layers, just make a mental note of it and move on with examining the inner layers.

What exactly are we looking for here? This can depend a lot on how your psychic senses perceive energy, but there are some typical patterns that I find are consistent with curses. First, if you've been good about regularly checking in with your body and know it well, then you should be able to notice if something in your auric field shouldn't be there. As a visual person this usually looks very obvious to me. On one of the few occasions where someone successfully threw a curse at me that stuck, it looked like a grey, gelatinous blob with little barbed spikes on its edges. The barbs were piercing the outer field of my aura like it was trying to penetrate it. This vision was very memorable because it reminded me of the way a virus looks when it's trying to infect different parts of the body and spread itself around. You might also notice cords (as we've already discussed in the body chapter), cracks, or holes that have a vacuum-like movement pattern, pulling your energy out of the body. Some people may actually see a vision of the person who cast the curse.

Next, perform the soul alignment exercise outlined in the body chapter. Aligning the souls helps to bring us back to a state that's the most 'us' we can be. After you perform the soul alignment, go back through the process of psychically examining the energy bodies from outside in. Does anything look different or is the issue still fully present? In my experience, if the issue you detected either disappeared entirely or was greatly lessened, then the issue is most likely something you generated yourself or otherwise simply stepped into by accident. This part of the meditation is how I can often tell if my issue came from outside of myself.

You can now either end the meditation here or continue to examine other parts of your energy bodies as well as the three souls. If I'm being particularly thorough, I will examine all the way into my innermost self until I reach my very core, then extend my sight outwards.

Regardless of your findings or lack of findings, keep a record of your experience and repeat on additional days if necessary. This way you can chart changes in the energy bodies for better or for worse.

Naming the Attacker

Although not usually necessary, it can be helpful to know exactly who the attacker is so you can incorporate that knowledge into your future protective works. This may or may not include binding the attacker from further harm, depending on the situation along with your personal preference.

An old folkloric method of identifying the sender of a curse is to write down the name of every suspect (including one labeled 'unknown') on a small slip of paper and balling the paper up in a marble of mud. Place all the mud marbles into a container of water and wait. It's said that the first mud marble to dissolve and cause the paper to float to the top will give you the name of the attacker.

My favorite method of curse sender detection is a simple one. Write down the name of each suspect (including 'unknown' along with your OWN name) on a sheet of paper or a board, somewhat close together. Use a pendulum to see which name it's drawn to. I like this method because it uses the trace energy of the sender that's already on you as a sort of ID tracer.

If you're proficient in a specific method of divination such as tarot, runes, or scrying, those methods may be more helpful to you. Beware that it's often challenging to look at situations like this about one's own self in an objective way.

Folkloric Methods of Curse Removal

If you've confirmed that you've got a curse on you, whether from outside sources or your own doing, you can now proceed with taking it off. Just as there are probably thousands of ways to detect a curse, there are just as many to take them off. Let's talk about some traditional folk techniques first.

Pots and Pans: Copper pots aren't just a superior set of cookware! Copper deflects negative energy and it's believed that intentionally shining them up repeatedly can deflect a hex as its settling in.

Clothing: Turning your clothing inside out is an act of sympathetic magic to 'turn out' a curse and 'put it in a pinch' by letting a closed door squeeze your shirt by the hinges. In Serbia, it's believed that accidentally putting on your shirt inside out means that someone is missing you. Maybe this way the curse will miss you, too!

Onions: Onions are thought to absorb impure energies from their immediate environment. Cut an onion in half, place it in a glass jar, and keep it under or next to your bed. As you sleep, the onion is thought to soak up the curse like a sponge. An ancient Babylonian spell involves peeling an onion and throwing the peels into a fire while praying for the unraveling of the curse.

Tablets: From Turkey we have the technique of writing a prayer for curse reversal on a sheet of tin and throwing it in a well or keeping it in a safe place. One example of wording reads: 'Drive away the curse. If anyone attempts to harm me, may the curse be thrown back at them.' Simple and right to the point.

Iron: Cursing someone with the iron-based 'War Water' is a common hex technique in several traditions around the globe. To reverse this, Germans will place three iron rings (like jewelry or iron knots from a hardware store) into a jar of water for 24 hours. After the 24 hours is up, the water is drunk. Although I can't be certain, this seems to be an act of fortifying the self with the material used to attack the victim, so that one becomes immune to it.

Fried Curses: A curious practice from China instructs us on what to do if you come into contact with a cursed object. Grab the object with tongs and place it into highly heated oil, 'frying' away a curse.

Smelly Head Wash: Another curious (but less fun) Chinese practice involves washing away a curse by making an infusion of mugwort and garlic and washing the head with it. Rinse well to get that smell out afterwards.

Limes: An interesting hex-breaker from Malaysia involves bathing with limes and sipping the water that falls off the hair. Careful about getting that in your eyes, though!

Elm: Elm trees are known in many traditions to turn back malefic magic. In the pow-wow of the Pennsylvania Dutch, sticks are broken off an elm tree on Good Friday and bound in the shape of a cross with holy names written on it. It is thought that wherever the cross hangs, evil magic will be turned away.

Suggested Strategies for Curse Removal

If folkloric methods aren't your thing, your first step for curse removal is looking at all of the cleansing and clearing techniques in both the body chapter and the home chapter of this book. In many cases, simple clearing techniques such as smudging can clear away crossed conditions easily if they are not too strong or deeply ingrained. If a curse feels deeply embedded, most of the cleansing baths should be enough to strip it away.

If cleansing your own self and your surroundings doesn't seem like enough or you're trying those techniques and they don't seem to be working well over time, you can try standard spells for curse reversal.

Exercise: Making a Curse Reversal Candle

Curse reversal candles are easy to make and pack a powerful punch. They're designed to 'turn the curse upside down' and throw off its energy vibration enough to loosen the grip it has on the victim. This reversal candle spell is the one I use and I offer it frequently to clients and loved ones for its simplicity and because it is easy to find the ingredients.

Materials:
Large black candle
Small mirror, slightly larger than the base of the candle
Olive oil
Chili pepper (crushed)
Garlic powder

Before crafting the candle, you should perform a full cleansing on your home and body. I recommend a thorough uncrossing bath first. This will help clear away any obstacles in your path before touching the curse itself. While performing your cleansings, be mindful of stripping away foul energies sent to you by others, energies that you may have accidentally walked through, and energies you may have generated from within. This will ensure that your reversal candle is effective against any type of curse, whether foreign or domestic.

Next, empower each of your materials in whatever way you

prefer, such as imagining bright and golden light flowing from your hands into each one. You may also wish to pray over each item in a way customary to your specific path. Feel free to use the following as a generic empowerment incantation:

By the mirror and by the shield
I charge this blessed tool
Be a force within a field
to turn away both foe and ghoul.

Carve a double-headed arrow extending the full length of the candle, pointing up and down. This symbolizes that the curse will be targeted from any direction that it's hitting you from and will be turned back to wherever it came from.

Now it's time to dress the candle. Olive oil serves to both draw in the energy of peace that the olive tree represents to humanity and to also serve as a sticking agent for your plant ingredients. Starting in the middle, rub the olive oil from the center of the candle to the bottom and then from the center of the candle to the top. This works to turn the offending energy away from inside out. To add the crushed pepper and garlic powder, you can simply roll the candle in the mixture, which should cover it nicely. Some people also like to carve small caverns into the candle's sides and stuff the plant matter in that way.

Lay the mirror flat with the reflective part facing upwards. Place the candle on top of that while you gently cradle it in your hands and activate it for your specific purpose.

Begin by mentally reviewing everything that has happened that you suspect is related to the curse. As you do, imagine the scene in your mind's eye shattering with a lightning bolt of bright, golden light. As it shatters, imagine that it is sucked up like a funnel and shot back into the void of the universe, like a black hole in space. This is when you would traditionally imagine your attacker, with the funnel of power being sent right back at them. I prefer most times to send the curse into the void while knowing that the universe will send it where it needs to go. Sometimes it's not always in our own best interest to send it back to the attacker for whatever reason. And sometimes we just simply don't know who the attacker is. Finally, I remind you that what you feel is a curse is sometimes your own doing, and you most certainly wouldn't want to send it back to yourself!

Light the candle and imagine as you do that a circle of mirrors encircles your body. The mirrors are simultaneously extracting any curse energy left over after the visualization while preventing what you've stripped away from coming back to you. As you visualize the mirrors shining brightly around, above, and below you, say:

By the mirror and by the shield
remove, hold, turn, reverse
Be a force within a field
and send away this foul curse!

By the mirror and by the shield
I banish, bind, and cross
Be a force within a field
above, below, across

By the mirror and by the shield
encircle me with light
Be a force within a field
to set this curse aflight!

You now have a couple options of what to do with the burning candle. You can either let it burn all the way down in one go, or you can light it every day for some specific length of time. I prefer the former method for the simple reason that I don't want to think about having to light the candle every single day. If you have a large candle and go this route, you must practice caution as it's likely that you'll need to allow it to burn overnight. For overnight candle burning, I use extra caution by placing the entire spell in a four-sided cooking pan that's part-filled with water. Then I'll put the pan with the spell inside my bathtub with the shower curtain tied away from the sides. This is perhaps a little paranoid, but I know that there's basically no chance of a fire being started with a candle burning inside a container of water in my bathtub. Don't do this if your bathtub is made of plastic though. As always, use common sense for your individual needs.

There is nothing more for you to do on the mystical side after the candle is lit. Just let it burn and try to not think about the curse or what's happening to it. While the candle is burning and for at least a few weeks after, you should strive to keep yourself as 'clean' as possible. Stay away from gossip, engaging in attacks, or triggering unnecessary aggression in others. If the curse was particularly bad, you may also want to follow up with regular uncrossing baths. In severe cases you may perform the uncrossing bath every night for seven nights after the initial lighting of the candle.

Exercise: Making a Mirror Box

Mirror boxes are a beloved method of curse reversal employed by many traditions. The idea is that the alleged attacker or the suspected origin of the attack is sealed away with their own cruel intentions until the attacks on you cease. This is a good working for when you are sure you know who the human attacker is or if you're sure you know how you became crossed up.

Materials:

A small, sturdy box of any kind (wooden boxes from craft stores work well)

Small craft mirrors (or cards of a larger mirror, broken up)

Salt
A token representing the attacker

The token can be one of several types of things. The best would be a lock of hair or fingernails from the person, however, it is usually rare for someone to have access to those things without living with the person. After that, the person's handwriting would make a powerful token as well. If none of those things are available, then a recent photo of the person will do. You may even wish to combine several objects. The token represents a psychic link and will forge the sympathetic connection to the attacker. In other words, what is done to the token in the spiritual world will affect the person in the physical

As with the curse reversal candle exercise, you'll want to perform a full personal and environmental cleansing in the same way. And, as with the candle spell, empower each item before you. You can use the same incantation:

By the mirror and by the shield
I charge this blessed tool
Be a force within a field
To turn away both foe and ghoul.

Glue the mirrors to the inside of the box on as many sides as you can. The reflective sides of the mirrors should face the inside, with the reflection of the token caught within it. If you're using a photo, place it so that the target's eyes are facing down. Scoop spoonfuls of salt over the token until it's buried. Salt is the neutralizer of the working and will shatter any hold the enemy attacker has on you.

Place your hands over the salt-filled box (with the box still open) and imagine silver light flowing into the mirrors. As you do this, you can say:

Box of reflection, salt of deflection
let this charm grant my protection
and hold within this chamber still
My enemy's malefic will.

Slam the box shut and then seal it in some way so that its contents won't be in danger of spilling out. I like to pour hot candle wax along the edges of the box. You can use superglue if you want to be thorough.

There is much debate in the mystical community about what should be done with these boxes when you're done. Some believe that like a witch bottle, the box should remain on your property to intercept any future attempts of attack on your person. Others will take it away from the property and bury it somewhere. This is my preferred method and I will add to that burying it at a crossroads if I can. I like the idea of the elements of nature disposing of the curse slowly for me.

Ancestral Curses and Bloodlines with Baggage

When I mentioned the 'psychic' con artists who tell people that they have curses on them that can be removed for a hefty fee, this often includes the explanation that the victim has entered a phase of an ancient curse that has been on their family for a very long time. This is insurance for the fraudulent seer because they can still make a claim on the curse without needing validation that it's an actual, living person that the victim knows. 'Your great-great grandfather angered an old gypsy woman who placed a curse on your family to make sure you will always remain poor!' That's just the tip of the iceberg to the type of claims made.

While I think it's extremely rare for a curse like the one used in my example to have actually happened, it can happen sometimes. Nothing is impossible when mystic forces are at work. Instead, a more common type of ancestral 'curse' is one that the ancestor may have formed accidentally, usually through a lifetime of bad decisions, or a bout of bad luck that they never did anything about. As I've mentioned several times, we often make curses on ourselves when we get tangled up in foul energy and fail to cleanse it away properly. In some cases, this gets so bad that it can affect one's children down a line, even after the originator of the condition is long past.

A great (however unfortunate) example are men who are told that they have their 'daddy's temper'. Being a short fuse emotionally and physically is often excused away by mere genetics, when it's actually a failure of a person to take responsibility for their anger issues. However, I believe that we can inherit certain emotional traits from our ancestors that can influence the way we react to things. Just like genetic predispositions to alcoholism, we can have genetic predispositions set up for us by the actions of our bloodline that came before.

Another way this can manifest is from what I call 'ancestral baggage', or the garbage that our ancestors accrued during their lives that was never resolved and so gets passed on down the bloodline for untold generations.

Fortunately, it is a lot easier to heal these accidental ancestral curses and baggage than you might think. Our lives are our own. As such, our natural state is one of independence and sovereignty. For the same reason why it's hard for intentional curses to stick to a person, it's hard for ancestral baggage to hold onto a person after it's acknowledged. Our lives crave balance and wholeness and will revert to that state once we pave the way for it.

Exercise: Breaking an Ancestral Curse

Materials:
A white candle of any size

Just one white candle? See, I told you this would be easy! The bulk of this simple exercise is meditative, so you will need to enter your meditative state in the way that you're used to. Before the meditation, it can be helpful to write out exactly what you feel the issue is so that you will be precise and focused on what you want to accomplish.

While breathing slowly and deeply in your meditation, think about the details of what you feel is an ancestral curse or ancestral baggage. In your mind's eye, imagine specific scenes playing out from your memory of what's happened. Think of more recent things first and then move backwards in time until you can no longer remember anything. Light the candle and say:

This burning flame I light in my name, [say your name]
I kindle the present and call forth the past.
Beloved ancestors, hear me.

Next, close your eyes and imagine that the energy of the curse is chipping away from your energy bodies, like ash does when it loosens up from burning wood and drifts away. As it detaches, see the fragments of the ancestral curse gathering towards the flame of the candle. The ancestral flame kindled holds a magnetic affect, pulling away all that's impure and not aligned with your own individual nature. Imagine this for several minutes until you can no longer see any fragments pulling away and drifting towards the flame. Now say this or another similar affirmation proclaiming that you are free of this:

In the name of past, present and future
I claim my present being!
May the ancestral flame burn away all that does not serve me
May the ancestral flame heal the past and make for the future
May the ancestral flame stay kindled in the hearth of my heart.
So must it be!

At the end of 'so must it be!' imagine any hovering curse fragments getting sucked up into the flame and at the same time, blow out the candle in one blow. Perform the soul alignment exercise to come back into your own being fully.

For some, this exercise is enough when worked one time. For others, it may take you several sessions. Even with nothing notable going on, I try to perform a variation of this about once a year or so, just in case I've come across anything that remains to be healed.

Prevention: The Best Medicine

I've said it before and I'll leave this with you again just to reinforce it: cleansing and clearing on a regular basis should be enough to ward away most curses, hexes, and crossed conditions most of the time. A regular cleansing practice is good spiritual hygiene and will help keep you from even having to deal with the material in this chapter. Although many curses can be dealt with in a speedy manner, some are a pain to deal with and can take time to recover from.

No one likes going to the dentist, so let's think of it in this way. Curse reversal can end up like dental surgery whereas a good regular cleaning could have prevented the need for it. We can't always keep ourselves free from debris and infection, but a good effort can keep us right a good deal of the time.

Chapter 5

Entities

The mystic is never alone in the work to infuse the world in spirit. And I don't just mean human company. The magic-worker, witch, and shaman all have a few things in common, but their most striking similarity in my eyes is in the form of entities. The mystic is often a bridge between this world and the next and learns the ability to communicate with beings in the beyond as well as beings in the present who we can't always perceive of with our usual senses. This can include entities who are friendly, unfriendly, or simply apathetic about our existence. It is one of the tasks of the mystic to perceive the difference between them. In his book *Spirit Allies: Meet Your Team from the Other Side*, author Christopher Penczak has this to say about the importance of entity work:

> *There are wise men and women in every culture who work with the unseen. The witches of Europe take much of their tradition from the priests and priestesses of the ancient lands of Egypt, Greece, India, and Gaul. They speak to spirits and gods to lean the future and perform magic. Modern witches are reclaiming these traditions. Spirit work comes in any spiritual context, from Christian mystics working with patron saints to the magi of the Hebrews, like King Solomon, who were great sorcerers. All in one form or another worked with the unseen realms... In these constants we find the threads of truth to weave our own experiences.*

In this chapter I'm going to take you on a guided tour through the various types of beings the mystic can encounter or call upon in the work of cleansing. We'll look at beings unfriendly (so you're better prepared to deal with them), friendly (so you can seek out possible allyships), and apathetic.

Allies and the Witch's Familiar

My good friend Patrick, a witch and practicing medium, is often quick to remind me that: 'Our first priority when dealing with the spirit should always be forming helpful relationships with spirits to protect our way forward.'

Entity allies not only help to keep us safe when working with other spirits who we're not yet familiar with, but they also add their own strength and focus to our work as mystics and healers.

A great example of spiritual allies can be found in my own personal tradition of witchcraft. The idea of the witch's familiar became a popular one in medieval times when inquisitors sought to connect the crimes of the witch to locations far away from the victim. It was thought that the witch sent out a familiar spirit in the form of an animal or some kind of beastly demon to perform their bidding. While the outrageous accusations of the witch trials are far behind us, we can still look to the bits of possible truth in the witch's art of gaining a familiar aid to help us in our work.

If you ask three witches what a familiar is you will get 10 answers. Different traditions hold different ideas for what exactly the familiar is. The common misconception among new practitioners is that a familiar is simply a witch's physical pet who lends their energy to a ritual. While that can be the case for some, a proper witch familiar is so much more. Here's a summary of the different types of familiars most often worked with in modern witchcraft:

Physical Animal Familiar: This is often a witch's pet who they work to develop a tight magical bond with. It's important to note that just because you're a witch with a pet, it doesn't automatically mean that the animal is your familiar. Physical animal familiars often choose whether to become so with their person and the witch has to make an effort to reach out to the animal through energetic means to make that happen.

Spirit Animal Familiar: This is the most common type of familiar worked with and is often to easiest to conjure up. Animal spirits are often very willing to work with witches and form a close bond because they're familiar with human nature and generally know what to expect of us. Often a spirit animal familiar is actually a strange, chthonic being that was previously formless, but takes the shape of an animal so that the witch will recognize it and better understand it. In the old witch trials, this often came up in the form of a witch being accused of sending their familiar for some task 'in the form of' a cat, bird, dog, snake, etc.

Plant Spirit Familiar: Similar to the animal spirit, this spirit arises from the collective consciousness of a specific type of plant or tree. It tends to be rare for a plant spirit to proactively approach the witch on its own and these familiar spirits are usually befriended by way of cultivating the physical plant and growing a spirit relationship over time.

Intelligent Thoughtform Familiar: This type of familiar is different from all the rest in that it is entirely created by the witch's own power, using their own life-force energy. The advantage of this thoughtform is that it's easier to give tasks to and tends to be more precise and easier to communicate with (since it's made of your own spiritual DNA). The downside is that it lacks congress with the other spirits of the beyond and of nature since it's a newly-created being.

Some might say that the true familiar spirit is a combination of all these things and more. Some think it's important to denote the differences. The technique below is designed to conjure up a familiar spirit that may take the shape of an animal, a plant, a human, or any combination of the above.

Exercise: Conjuring the Familiar Spirit

Enter a meditative state in the manner of your choosing, including some sort of temple erection, if only a circle casting at the least. Since you are reaching out into the void of the spirit world, the basic protections that the circle provides will be valuable.

To awaken your wild and ecstatic state, sway or dance, slowly at first and then rapidly. Drum beats or other rapid music can help with this, and moderate amounts of alcohol can as well (but don't overdo the latter while in ritual state as you will need to be able to discern between spirits and hallucinations).

On a sheet of paper or a canvass, draw or paint this seal:

1. Three concentric circles representing land, sea, and sky.
2. The rune algiz, which is one vertical line that branches out at the top with three smaller lines (look up this rune online if you're unsure). Algiz represents spirit guardianship.
3. On the left side of the rune, a clockwise spiral.
4. On the right side of the rune, a five-pointed star.

As you design the seal, continue to breath slow and deep while swaying or chanting.

With your will, call out into the void of space and time and mentally ask for a spirit familiar to appear before you as a willing assistant. Take your time with this and don't limit yourself by material expectations as it may not come in a form you are familiar with. Allow it to fully manifest before your mind's eye and take note of its appearance and any name it may present to you.

When done, stare at the seal, close your eyes, and imagine it in your mind's eye. When you have a solid visualization going, loudly speak the invocation to call forth the spirit familiar into the physical world:

Seal and sigil born this day
awaken to this mystic's word
Stand before me, strong and stay
as if a stag or hare or bird

Next, hold the seal over the candle flame so that it is warmed yet not burned. Imagine that the power of the flame enters the seal, along with your own vital life force energy. The giving of this energy relates to the historical idea of the witch's familiar suckling on the life-force of the witch to birth it into the physical world. You should strain to pour an enormous amount of power into the seal so that it's a true offering. When you feel this has been accomplished, speak the invocation of confirmation:

Flame to pierce the sigil's flesh
Warmth to nurture at my breast
Suckled in creator's arms
and given life unto this charm.
I give you life!

At this point you should spend some time in meditation with the familiar, giving it instructions or general intentions on what you plan to do with it. Will it mostly be used to deliver magical goals to others? Will it act as an ambassador to other spirits? Will it guard your home while inside it and your body while you travel? Anything you can think of that a powerful spirit-being could do for you, you should make known now. Some people also like to specify with the spirit that they are not to do anything on their behalf unless specifically instructed to do so.

Once this is done, wrap the seal of the familiar spirit in cloth and store it in some safe space. Only expose the seal to the air when you are calling forth or sending away the familiar.

Later when you need to call the spirit for some task, trace your fingers over the seal on the paper as you say:

(Name, if known), I call you here
with words that fall upon thy ear.

When done with the spirit, send it away in the same way but by saying:

(Name, if known), I license thee to now depart
with gratitude and loving heart.

Clearing with the Familiar

With a relationship to a familiar formed, you can now ask of it just about anything, whether cleansing related or not. One of my favorite things to do with a familiar spirit is to clear a room or building ahead of time before I even get there. Since many of the space clearing workings in this book require you to be physically present in some way, being able to pre-clear a space can be helpful for any number of reasons. In particular, I've taught this method to mystical friends who are involved with ghost hunting work and are responsible for clearing away potentially harmful entities before the rest of the crew goes into a space. Being able to send in your familiar allows you to remain safely within the confines of your own space while the spirit happily performs the heavy lifting.

To send out your familiar, use the exercise above and explain to it exactly what you need to accomplish. This can be in the context of a larger ritual working or not. I will usually incorporate at least some kind of physical action to empower the familiar and send along my own energetic impressions. For example, let's use the ghost hunting example. Let's say that a group has asked me to clear away a particularly nasty spirit that is thought to be inside a home inhabited by many other spirits that they wish to document. I would call up the spirit and write down the address of the house and maybe even add a photo to go along with it. While explaining to my familiar the issue and how I need its help, I would burn the paper while praying for the final outcome. I might also chant repeatedly to send the spirit out with my own added energy with some simple words like: 'Away, away, familiar spirit, send the foul spirit away...' Over time and with regular contact, you'll start to develop a specific relationship with your familiar and know more about what to do to send it out.

Now that the familiar spirit is in your life, it needs to be periodically fed. To do this you can pour life-force energy into the seal like you did in the initial conjuration exercise. You may also wish to call it into being at a specific time like the full moon and leave it an offering of alcohol (spirits to feed the spirits!).

Consider the ongoing relationship with your familiar to be a work in progress that will grow over time. Over time, it will let you know more about itself and you will both come to trust one another. In truth, the spirit familiar is part of your essence as its movement in the physical world is partly reliant on your feeding of it.

Ancestral Helpers

In previous chapters we discussed the power of ancestral energy and how the lives of those who lived before can affect us today. While in the curse chapter we were focused on healing the trauma of the past, the ancestors should be considered in your proactive cleansing needs for present situations as well.

As entities, the ancestors have the specific trait of being particularly interested in our human needs. Whereas an angelic being is usually going to be concerned with our higher evolution or the gaining of wisdom, your dear old great grandmother is more likely to be concerned with getting you a raise or a new boyfriend.

I'm not going to give you a specific ritual working to call in the ancestors. The best ritual for forging a spiritual relationship with your ancestors is to work with them constantly in your personal spiritual practice. This means physically saying their names, including them in your prayers, and speaking to them directly.

Your personal relationships with your ancestors depends on a couple of different factors. First, you should know that while human spirits often become more enlightened once they experience death and move into the otherworld, they still retain much of their worldly personality. So if your crazy uncle was never quite able to hold down a job because of reckless behavior, you may want to choose a different ancestor to help you get that promotion. If your deceased cousin was the best baker in town, don't be afraid to ask for some help before that church bake sale. And if your dad was always the tidiest one in the family, he's probably going to be one of your go-to contacts for ancestral cleansing.

The other factor that affects your ancestral relationships can be your relationship with them while they were alive. While you absolutely can and should work with ancestors both named and unnamed who stretch back into the echoes of time, most people find it easier to forge relationships with those they actually knew. The bonds of that love and the experience of growing physically with someone while here on the physical plane form a powerful bond that remains strong after they leave us.

In the practical sense, you can ask the ancestors for help for similar reasons that you might ask a familiar spirit. The difference is that, unlike the familiar spirit, you are not going to compel and direct the ancestors to do what you want in your place. Instead, the ancestors should be pleaded to for favors, just like you'd ask for a favor from a living family member. If you ask that cousin for baking help and have never so much as uttered a word of honor to her name, she might not be willing to step in.

Ancestral relationships should be reciprocal. They benefit from our remembrance of them (which empowers their spirits and propels them into positive karmic states) and we benefit from the influence they hold in the spiritual realm.

Aside from rites performed entirely around the ancestors on their own, you can incorporate them into other work you're doing. For example, you might add on an ancestral blessing to your uncrossing bath by saying for example *'By Grandma Jean and the power of my ancestors, may this water be blessed.'*

Angels

We all know who angels are in general, but you may not know that they're one of the most common entities across nearly all religions and forms of mysticism. From the Old English (and before that, borrowed from Greek), the word angel means 'messenger' and that's probably the best title they could have. Angels are messengers between this physical world and the upper, heavenly realms. In certain traditions of modern shamanism this might be called the 'upper world' or the part of reality that holds the powers that are more light and airy, yet sometimes blindingly harsh with truth.

In the Abrahamic religions, angels are often seen as fierce and even sometimes terrifying beings. The Bible contains all kinds of disturbing accounts of people being blinded and killed by angels. It also has some inspiring stories about angels coming to the aid of humanity and helping to conquer evil. It even seems that we might have our own personal angels, sent by the divine to specifically look after us:

For he shall give his angels charge over thee, to keep thee in all thy ways. They shall bear thee up in [their] hands, lest thou dash thy foot against a stone. Thou shalt tread upon the lion and adder: the young lion and the dragon shalt thou trample under feet.
Psalms 91:11

Angels don't just belong to the Abrahamic faiths, though. Even my own tradition of witchcraft has angelic lore in the form of the Nephilim, angelic beings that are the result of the high angels mating with humans and giving birth to these magical, giant-like beings (who also mate with humans, producing the first witches):

> *The Nephilim were in the earth in those days; and also after that, when the sons of God came in unto the daughters of men, and they bare [children] to them, the same [became] mighty men which [were] of old, men of renown.*
> Genesis 6:4

We find angels featured even more prominently in the high magic traditions such as Qabalah and Enochian (the former of which is based entirely on angelic visions and language). Angels bridge the gap between the world's faiths and spiritual traditions.

As the messengers of the divine, angels make fantastic entities to partner with for cleansing work. I was taught that the energetic vibration of angels is so high, no low vibrational dark energy can exist when they are intentionally near. I say intentionally because I was also taught that angels don't intervene in ordinary human affairs unless specifically asked to do so. I have found that to be the case in my own work, as I never seem to sense the presence of angelic beings unless I specifically call out to them for help or assistance. As with any mystical endeavor, you should let your own experience guide the way, but I always recommend intentionally calling out to a type of entity regularly if you seek their continued support.

Asking for the support of angels is something I find to be extremely straightforward. They don't seem to require offerings like certain gods, spirits, or even some ancestors. Instead, I have found that anything you can do to connect your goal with some higher purpose will cause them to be more willing to lend a hand. For example, you might feel that cleansing your own body of destructive energy is essential for your pursuit of wisdom and universal love. That's just the type of thing the angelic beings like to hear.

Exercise: An Angelic Cleansing

This simple exercise is a basic method for calling up the angelic powers for cleansing work. I have framed it around the clearing of space, although you could easily adapt this to almost any other type of cleansing work.

Materials:
A white candle
A found feather

Enter a meditative state in your usual preferred method and then immediately light the wick of your candle. As it ignites, focus strongly on the flame itself and the aura of light that surrounds it. See the halo in the flame and take note of its feathery, soft texture.

In your mind's eye, imagine that the flame whips up and forms enormous flaming wings before you. Imagine that attached to these wings, an angelic being materializes before you, shining with light that's almost too bright for you to bear. Acknowledge its presence with a nod or a bow and state very simply what your goal is for the working and that you require its assistance.

Take up your feather (make sure you sanitize it first!) in one hand and the candle in the other. Walk around the space with the candle and hold it in every area you can so that the light for the candle touches every single nook and cranny of the space. Use the feather to fan the flame of the candle, imagining as you do that additional light is flooding into the space from the candle. As you walk, imagine the angelic being walking with you every step of the way, touching the parts of the space as the light of the candle touches it.

When you've reached every space, blow out the candle and say your own words of thanks to the angelic being.

Gods, Goddesses, and Divine Beings

I wrote this book to appeal to many aspects of mysticism, which may or may not include the belief in various gods and other numinous divine beings. Regardless, I must include the gods because their presence would be starkly missed in a book that seeks to purify the body and space by way of spiritual power. There are many variations of belief in the gods that can even include the idea that the gods were merely manifestations of energy in the collective minds. Even though I consider them to be actual sovereign entities with their own unique personas, their power and oversight can still be invaluable.

I prefer to always include the gods and divine beings into my cleansing work in some way, if only in a brief prayer asking them to guard my way. If you already have some kind of devotional practice to divine beings, you should certainly consider carrying that into the work of spiritual cleansing. Here are a few examples of how I incorporate pleas to the gods in my work:

Prayer: Although I believe prayer should always be coupled with action, prayer on its own is an invaluable tool to help keep you open to insights about what you're doing. I always insist that half the challenge in prayer work is listening. When you're constantly open to communication with the overarching divine powers, it can be a lot easier to reach other entities as well.

Altars and Shrines: If you have some kind of cleansing altar (even if it's only temporary), place icons of the gods (or 'God' singularly, if you're a monotheist) alongside your tools. Images of the gods refresh us and remind us of the greater good as we set up the physical structures for our work.

Full Rituals: When performing a multi-step cleansing ceremony that makes up an entire ritual, it's helpful to include the gods as a way to focus and contain your work. Additionally, the insight of the gods can go a long way in stretching your will towards the final goal if you weren't able to raise quite enough energy for whatever you're doing. An example of this would be performing a home clearing exercise while sick. Since you might be at a physical disadvantage due to illness, the gods with their unlimited outside influence can push your work to the needed end mark.

Human Spirits

I like to specify 'human spirits' when talking about people since 'spirit' can be any number of vast beings out there in the other-world. Although the issue of trapped or bothersome human spirits is one of the more uncommon issues you'll encounter in day-to-day cleansing work, it's one of the most common questions I receive as a mystic and a magic-worker. Everyone thinks they're haunted. But who exactly are these 'ghosts', what do they want, and how should we handle them when encountered? First, we need to point out the difference between the two. Ghosts and human spirits are not the same.

Although this can be debated, human spirits are part of the actual spiritual essence of a real human being after their current physical incarnation has died. In this way, I would classify an ancestor who graces the physical realm as a human spirit. While human spirits trapped here unintentionally (or worse, on purpose) are a popular idea thanks to Hollywood, it's not a very common thing you'll experience. Human spirits who actually become trapped here by way of unfinished business are often quite easy to send away. Most of the time they just need an exit and a reason to leave. Many don't even know it's possible to leave! The following is one of the simplest exercises in this entire book. If you thought banishing a discarnate human spirit was going to be the most dramatic and dangerous thing to learn in this book, I apologize in advance for disappointing you!

Exercise: Setting a Human Spirit Free

Before performing this working, I find it extraordinarily helpful to make contact with the spirit to make sure it's not actually a ghost (which we'll cover next) and to make it aware of what's actually going on. While spirit communication can often be filled with a variety of complex methods of operation, covering such things is far beyond the scope of this book. If you're unfamiliar with formalized methods of spirit communication, at least enter a meditative state, say a protective prayer, and reach out to the spirit mentally using pure intention alone. Sometimes that's all you need. Remember that not all human spirits want to leave just yet, and that's okay. Obviously, if the spirit is endangering you or your family, you can insist that it depart.

Materials:
A white or blue candle
Stick of incense (cedar is best, but any will do)

Whether this is your first time communicating with the spirit or not, go into your meditative state and attempt to make contact with the spirit once again. Explain that it's a trapped, human spirit and that there is a better world beyond where it can find peace and completion. Assure the spirit that there is nothing to fear and that you approach it with the love and trust of the divine.

Make sure you have performed some kind of space protection working, even as simple as using your mind to project a sphere of shining blue light around you. You may also wish to call in the archangel Michael who is excellent with sending spirits on their way.

Hold the candle, light it and focus on the halo of light that surrounds the flame. Place the candle on the ground before you, still focusing on the halo, and imagine that halo getting bigger and brighter. It grows so large that it forms into the shape of a brilliant, shining doorway before you. Say the following:

Sacred flame upon the floor
arise at once to make a door!
Part the veil to spirit realm
and heed the words upon the helm!
And filter all I don't allow
from passing through the doorway's bow.

Light the incense and place it before the candle, to lure the spirit to the door with its pleasing scent. Allow as much time as you need to feel the spirit approaching. If you have trouble sensing the spirit, then give yourself about 12 slow breaths before moving on. When ready, say:

Smoke is the gift of air and upon its wings you fly
Oh spirit must you cross this door and pass this world by.

Again, take your time in attempting to sense if the spirit leaves or not. If it does, then you're ready to close the door. If not, then you may wish to wait until another time to try or the spirit may not want to leave. If it doesn't want to leave then you can proceed to the next exercise in this chapter: Casting Out an Entity. To close the door, imagine that the doorway shrinks back down to the candle base until it is once again just a small halo of light. Blow out the candle. It is done.

You should then perform some kind of basic space clearing to tidy up any residual energy. And that's it!

Ghosts

While most people assume that a ghost is just another name for a discarnate human spirit, that's not the case. What many mystics actually call 'ghosts' are really echoes of a person, place, or event's energy or memory imprint.

When dramatic, terrifying, or even joyful events occur, they can imprint themselves on a space with their energy. This usually happens when an event was so strong, the normal energy of the space can't even contain and process what it's experiencing all at once. As a result, the event is 'absorbed' into the energetic pores of the area.

When someone is experiencing a 'haunting' what they're usually experiencing is an echo playing itself out over and over again. It's easy to confuse this with the actions of a discarnate human spirit because the ghost's actions can seem either totally random, or highly intentional and meant to frighten the human observer. While hauntings don't often have intelligent influence behind them, that doesn't make them any less of an unnerving experience, especially when the visions, sounds, smells, etc. are unpleasant. When a haunting is unwanted, you can clear it away by disconnecting the energy echo from the physical space and purifying the space so it can't repeat.

Often, performing basic spiritual hygiene on an area is enough to unplug that energy and send the ghosts packing. Most often when I encounter a so-called 'haunted house', I can clear away that energy signature with something as basic as a cedar stick smudging in about 20 minutes.

Some hauntings are not so easily moved. These can include times when a space is poisoned by a terrible tragedy such as a murder, suicide, loss of a child, or even (as I've experienced once before) the announcement of a divorce that happened 50 years prior! In those cases, here are a few things you could incorporate into a space clearing to deal with a difficult haunting:

- Regularly burn herbs that deal with clearing away the past and any associated spirits. You can also incorporate them into floor washes and sprays. Suggested herbs for this include: Asafetida, mugwort, wormwood, rosemary, rue, angelica, and copal.
- 'Overwrite' the echo by creating your own! If the haunting is happening in a particular area of a house, intentionally create new memories there on a regular basis. Plan a party, announce good news, and fill the space with all of your favorite things.
- Fill the room with as much light as you can. Sunlight neutralizes and sterilizes energetic memories in many cases. Adding artificial lights like lamps can also help you to associate the area with a 'bright and happy' space.
- Conjure up a familiar spirit and ask it to work away at clearing the space as a long-term project.
- Encircle the room with quartz crystals. Quartz vibrates at such a high frequency, it's difficult for hauntings to remain in place while the stones emit their own vibrations. You'd be amazed at the success some people have with placing a few quartz stones around a room and charging them regularly while there.

Demons, Ghouls, and Other Nasties

I hesitated on even mentioning intentionally harmful entities in here because of how rare they are to encounter. I never want to enforce something like this as a go-to explanation for a troublesome experience. Because of the fear tactics of certain Abrahamic schools of thought, many of us have been told that there are demons lurking around every corner and the tiniest slip up can cause you to become attacked, possessed, or worse. Your first step in becoming safe from these dark denizens is to stop, take a breath, and shake off that fear! The chance of encountering something as dramatic as a legitimately dangerous and intentionally harmful entity is (in this mystic's opinion) akin to being the victim of an armed robbery.

This is where the power of discernment comes in. If you fear that a haunting is putting you in danger and that there may be an intelligent force behind it, you must first diagnose its true nature. Misdiagnosing a haunting (or worse, your own self-induced curse) as a demonic presence can make your situation worse. Perform a divination, seek the assistance of your helpful entities, or otherwise employ whatever insightful methods of information gathering you can.

In the rare occasion that you do encounter such a beast (and at worst, this might be an aggressive human spirit), here are the steps I recommend you take:

1. Perform what you feel is the most powerful bodily cleansing you can, followed by what you feel is the most powerful space clearing ritual you have.
2. Protection! Employ your preferred methods to accumulate a strong protective presence, both through your own energetic techniques and through the aid of your helpful entities. When dealing with an offending entity, I prefer to call up my familiar spirit to act as a personal bodyguard. The ancestors are often extremely helpful with this as well, especially if you have a loved one who was highly protective of you.
3. Fire a 'warning shot'. While in your sacred space, demand that the being leave immediately. Warn it that if it does not leave you by your specified time, you will banish it to the furthest depths of the otherworld where it will forever be bound for all eternity. Make your threat dramatic! Which brings us to our final exercise...

Exercise: Casting Out an Entity

Materials:
Incense charcoal for burning herbs
Broom
These plants, powdered: Asafetida, garlic, sage, chili pepper, bay leaf
Holy water

Prepare your space by performing a full-body cleansing and a complete space clearing. Ignite the charcoal now so it has a chance to heat up. Cast a circle of protection around your working area by walking around it three times, imagining as you do that a shining blue flame erupts at the edge. The flame rises up and encompasses your whole area, with you in the center of the large sphere. Affirm the casting by pounding on the ground three times, saying:

Here with might and magic stand, heart to heart and hand in hand
mark oh powers and here me now, affirming this my sacred vow.
That naught but good shall enter forth
by east to south to west to north!
So must it be!

Hold your hands over the ground up plant mixture and charge them with golden light and say:

Spirits of the herbs of exorcism, awaken and come forth!
Let the sun be made pale by your presence.
Let the garden of life lend its gifts to my work.
Let the evil present be ensnared by your tendrils and cast out!

Pour the mix onto the smoldering coals and allow the thick and foul-scented smoke to rise. Carry the burning potion to all corners of the space while you chant:

> *By Michael and Gabriel, by Uriel and Raphael*
> *I cast the evil being out by the might of the angelic powers!*
> *By the ancestors of the past and descendants of the future*
> *I cast the evil being out by the might of the blood within me!*
> *By the leaf and the bud, the blossom and vine*
> *I cast the evil being out by the might of the powers of earth!*

When the smoke has reached all areas, return the burning mixture to your working area and take up your besom. Hold it tight in your hands and imagine that the brush part of it becomes engulfed in blue flames that sizzle and crack in the air. Breathe power into the besom until the flame can hardly be contained any longer. Then take the besom around the area and begin sweeping, from east to west. As you do, imagine the blue flame of the brush incinerating the air before you, purifying it of all things cruel, foul, and fell. As you do this, YELL the following as loud as you're able:

> *By handle and brush of the witch's broom*
> *I cast the evil being out by the holy powers of the blue flame of faery!*
> *Evil being, hear me:*
> *I cast you out by the light inside me!*
> *I cast you out by the strength inside me!*
> *I cast you out by the guardians around me!*
> *I cast you out by the nexus and the void!*
> *I cast you out! I cast you out! I cast you out!*
> *Be gone!*

Return to your working space and take some deep, cleansing breaths. All your energy should ground and become tempered as you feel the energy of the space shift and lighten, now that the entity has been evicted.

Finally, sprinkle holy water in all areas of the space, on your body, and on your tools. Take an uncrossing bath and then reinforce your personal protections around your home in a way appropriate for you.

In Conclusion

While this slim volume may not have the answer to every obstacle you face in life, I hope it has helped to clear the way for you to find some solutions. The work of cleansing and clearing is a lifelong pursuit and as long as we stand on this earth, we will always encounter things that muck up our energy or hold us back. That's a good thing! Facing challenges sometimes means that we've done some kind of work in the world. Resistance is natural, whether it comes from yourself or others.

As you go forth in making your world a cleaner place to live in, I ask that you do so knowing that this is a sacred work that the world truly needs. All of us who are willing to conjure up some peace, prosperity, and success are needed to make this planet a safer and more just place to live. May your work be blessed.

Blessed be,
David Salisbury

MOON
BOOKS

Moon Books invites you to begin or deepen your encounter with
Paganism, in all its rich, creative, flourishing forms.

If you have enjoyed this book, why not tell other readers by posting a review on your preferred booksite. Recent bestsellers from Moon Books are:

Journey to the Dark Goddess
How to Return to Your Soul
Jane Meredith
Discover the powerful secrets of the Dark Goddess and transform your depression, grief and pain into healing and integration.
Paperback: 978-1-84694-677-6
ebook: 978-1-78099-223-5

Shamanic Reiki
Expanded Ways of Working with Universal Life Force Energy
Llyn Roberts, Robert Levy
Shamanism and Reiki are each powerful ways of healing; together, their power multiplies. Shamanic Reiki introduces techniques to help healers and Reiki practitioners tap ancient healing wisdom.
Paperback: 978-1-84694-037-8
ebook: 978-1-84694-650-9

Pagan Portals – The Awen Alone
Walking the Path of the Solitary Druid
Joanna van der Hoeven
An introductory guide for the solitary Druid, *The Awen Alone* will accompany you as you explore and seek out your own place within the natural world.
Paperback: 978-1-78279-547-6
ebook: 978-1-78279-546-9

A Kitchen Witch's World of Magical Herbs & Plants

Rachel Patterson

A journey into the magical world of herbs and plants, filled with magical uses, folklore, history and practical magic. By popular writer, blogger and kitchen witch, Tansy Firedragon.

Paperback: 978-1-78279-621-3

ebook: 978-1-78279-620-6

Medicine for the Soul

The Complete Book of Shamanic Healing

Ross Heaven

All you will ever need to know about shamanic healing and how to become your own shaman...

Paperback: 978-1-78099-419-2

ebook: 978-1-78099-420-8

Shaman Pathways – The Druid Shaman

Exploring the Celtic Otherworld

Danu Forest

A practical guide to Celtic shamanism with exercises and techniques as well as traditional lore for exploring the Celtic Otherworld.

Paperback: 978-1-78099-615-8

ebook: 978-1-78099-616-5

Traditional Witchcraft for the Woods and Forests

A Witch's Guide to the Woodland with Guided Meditations and Pathworking

Melusine Draco

A Witch's guide to walking alone in the woods, with guided meditations and pathworking.

Paperback: 978-1-84694-803-9

ebook: 978-1-84694-804-6

Wild Earth, Wild Soul
A Manual for an Ecstatic Culture
Bill Pfeiffer
Imagine a nature-based culture so alive and so connected,
spreading like wildfire. This book is the first flame...
Paperback: 978-1-78099-187-0
ebook: 978-1-78099-188-7

Naming the Goddess
Trevor Greenfield
Naming the Goddess is written by more than 80 adherents and
scholars of the Goddess and Goddess Spirituality.
Paperback: 978-1-78279-476-9
ebook: 978-1-78279-475-2

Shapeshifting into Higher Consciousness
Heal and transform yourself and our world with ancient and
modern Shamanic methods.
Llyn Roberts
Ancient and modern methods that you can use every day
to transform yourself and make a positive difference in the
world.
Paperback: 978-1-84694-843-5
ebook: 978-1-84694-844-2

**Find more titles and sign up to our readers' newsletter at
http://www.johnhuntpublishing.com/paganism.
Follow us on Facebook at
https://www.facebook.com/MoonBooks and Twitter at
https://twitter.com/MoonBooksJHP. Most titles are
published in paperback and as an ebook. Paperbacks are
available in physical bookshops. Both print and ebook
editions are available online. Readers of ebooks can click
on the live links in the titles to order.**